Delicious & Dependable
Slow Cooker
Recipes

Delicious & Dependable
Slow Cooker Recipes

Judith Finlayson

Robert
ROSE

Delicious & Dependable Slow Cooker Recipes
Text copyright © 2002 Judith Finlayson
Photographs copyright © 2002 Robert Rose Inc.

For complete cataloguing information, see page 248.

Disclaimer
The recipes in this book have been carefully tested by our kitchen and our tasters. To the best of our knowledge, they are safe and nutritious for ordinary use and users. For those people with food or other allergies, or who have special food requirements or health issues, please read the suggested contents of each recipe carefully and determine whether or not they may create a problem for you. All recipes are used at the risk of the consumer.

We cannot be responsible for any hazards, loss or damage that may occur as a result of any recipe use.

For those with special needs, allergies, requirements or health problems, in the event of any doubt, please contact your medical adviser prior to the use of any recipe.

Design & Production: PageWave Graphics Inc.
Editor: Carol Sherman
Copy Editor: Julia Armstrong
Photography: Mark T. Shapiro
Food Stylist: Kate Bush
Props Stylist: Charlene Erricson
Color Scans: Colour Technologies

The publisher and author wish to express their appreciation to the following supplier of props used in the food photography:

DISHES, LINENS AND ACCESSORIES

Homefront
371 Eglinton Ave. W.
Toronto, Ontario, M5N 1A3
Tel: (416) 488-3189
www.homefrontshop.com

Pier 1 Imports
Toronto, Ontario

The Kitchen and Glass Place
840 Yonge St.
Toronto, Ontario, M4W 2H1
Tel: (416) 927-9925

FLATWARE

Gourmet Settings Inc.
245 West Beaver Creek Rd., Unit 10
Richmond Hill, Ontario, L4B 1L1
Tel: 1-800-551-2649
www.gourmetsettings.com

Cover image: Beef and Sausage Chili (see recipe, page 80)
Photo page 2: Meredith's Molten Blondies (see recipe, page 238)

We acknowledge the financial support of the Government of Canada through the Book Publishing Industry Development Program (BPIDP) for our publishing activities.

Published by: Robert Rose Inc.
120 Eglinton Ave. E., Suite 800, Toronto, Ontario, Canada M4P 1E2
Tel: (416) 322-6552 Fax: (416) 322-6936

Printed in Canada
2 3 4 5 6 7 8 9 10   FC   09 08 07 06 05

To Bob and Meredith

Acknowledgments

Since this book is a sequel, commissioned after my first slow cooker book achieved a gratifying degree of success, I find myself in the rather awkward position of thanking many of the same people all over again. How many ways can I say thank you to all of you who contributed so much?

Once again, the Robert Rose creative team went the extra mile to produce a great-looking and rigorously edited book. Bob Dees and Marian Jarkovich bring an outstanding attention to detail to all their projects and this one certainly benefited from all their painstakingness. We can all be proud of the results. Thanks to props stylist Charlene Erricson and food stylist Kate Bush for the great job they did in setting the visual stage; and, of course, to photographer Mark Shapiro, who, once again, brought the recipes to life on film. Designers Andrew Smith, Joseph Gisini and Kevin Cockburn at PageWave Graphics never cease to amaze me. Working quietly in the background, their attention to detail creates synergy among the individual contributions, ensuring that the whole becomes more than the sum of its parts.

I am also very fortunate to have Carol Sherman as my editor. Supportive, diligent and astute, she makes the editorial process fun, and I actually look forward to her questioning calls. Jennifer MacKenzie's enthusiasm and thoroughness puts the finishing touch on recipes. Tracking down missing modifiers and giving recipes a final test, she allows us all to breathe more easily in the final stages, before the book heads off to the printer.

I have also been blessed with a group of supportive friends and neighbors who love to cook. They often shared ideas with me and gallantly tasted my recipes in progress, even when they missed the mark. Special thanks are due to Audrey King, an excellent home cook with a "day job" as a symphony cellist. The insight and precision she brings to her career made a particularly beneficial contribution to this book.

And last, but certainly not least, my family. My husband, Bob, persuaded me to write my first cookbook, and I'm pleased that after more than 20 years together he continues to enjoy my cooking with great gusto. And, of course, my daughter, Meredith, a perceptive critic and appreciative audience, who is showing great promise as a cook.

Thanks to you all!

Contents

Introduction

Since writing my first slow cooker book, I've become even more convinced of the value of this amazing appliance. Not only is it a great convenience, it fits so well with the way I like to cook that it constantly inspires me to think of new ways to incorporate its services into my life. With this book, I've added more than 150 new recipes to my previous collection. These include numerous recipes for Fish and Seafood, Meatless Main courses and Desserts, as well as an abundance of meat and poultry dishes, which are more traditionally associated with the slow cooker. I've also increased the number of recipes that are suitable for vegetarians and have noted those in the upper right corner of the page when appropriate. As in my previous book, I've tried to include a wide range of recipes that will appeal to many tastes and requirements — from great family food to more sophisticated recipes for entertaining.

As a committed slow cooker fan, it doesn't surprise me that this versatile appliance, invented in the 1970s as a device for cooking beans, is enjoying a lively revival in the early years of the new millennium. Quite simply, it is one of the most effective time-management tools any cook can have. With its help, even the busiest people can regularly enjoy delicious home-cooked meals. Using the slow cooker, it's just as much fun to experiment with many exotic dishes that reflect the expanding horizons of home cooking in our global world as it is to recreate many of the more traditional dishes that were a meaningful part of the past.

Every culture and household has dishes that are remembered as "comfort food." In our multicultural society, these range from the kind of dishes my mother cooked, such as pot roast, baked beans and chicken stew with dumplings, to those I sampled at the homes of neighbors and friends. Among them was then unfamiliar fare such as lasagna, meatballs in tomato ragu and Chinese ribs. I have fond memories of these long-simmered, richly flavored dishes, which were an integral part of my growing up, and they are deeply linked with my sense of hearth and home.

I still love cooking these old-fashioned dishes, such as *Classic Beef Stew* or *Chicken 'n' Dumplings*, but I also love to experiment, developing more adventuresome recipes that draw on the many ingredients from around the world, readily available in supermarkets today. I particularly enjoy using herbs and spices in such dishes as *Wine-Braised Veal with Rosemary* and *Cumin-Flavored Black Bean Soup with Tomato*, and the many varieties of sausages that lend zest to dishes such as *Beef and Sausage Chili*. I've become quite smitten with the many kinds of chili peppers, both fresh and dried, that now turn up on supermarket shelves, and I love experimenting with these spicy condiments in such dishes as *African-Style Braised Chicken in Peanut Sauce* and *Short Ribs in Chili Sauce*.

There's more to using a slow cooker than putting food on the table. In my opinion, the meals it allows you to prepare nourish both body and soul. Made from fresh and wholesome ingredients, with levels of fat and salt controlled by the home cook, slow cooker dishes are certainly nutritious. But more than that, they offer a reassuring antidote to the stresses of our fast-paced, high-tech age. There are few experiences more pleasurable than arriving home to be greeted by the appetizing aroma of a simmering soup or stew, the kinds of dishes that the slow cooker excels at producing.

About six million slow cookers are sold every year. This makes it one of our most popular appliances, which isn't surprising since it is also one of the easiest to use. Once the food is in the slow cooker, you can usually forget about it until it's ready to serve. With the slow cooker's help, anyone can prepare delicious food with a minimum of attention and maximum certainty of success. I sincerely hope you will try these recipes and that you will enjoy them and make the slow cooker a regular part of your life.

— *Judith Finlayson*

Using Your Slow Cooker

An Effective Time Manager

In addition to producing great-tasting food, a slow cooker is one of the most effective time-management tools available. Once the ingredients have been prepared and assembled in the stoneware and the appliance is turned on, you can forget about it. The slow cooker performs unattended while you carry on with your workaday life. You can be away from the kitchen all day and return to a hot, delicious meal.

A Low-Tech Appliance

Slow cookers are amazingly low tech. The appliance usually consists of a metal casing and a stoneware insert with a tight-fitting lid. For convenience, this insert should be removable from the metal casing, making it easier to clean and increasing its versatility as a serving dish. The casing contains the heat source: electrical coils. These coils do their work using the energy it takes to power a 100-watt light bulb. Because the slow cooker operates on such a small amount of energy, you can safely leave it turned on while you are away from home.

Slow Cooker Basics

Slow cookers are generally round or oval and range in size from 1 to 7 quarts. The small round ones are ideal for dips and fondues, as well as some soups, main courses and desserts. The larger sizes, usually oval, are necessary to cook whole roasts of chickens and desserts that need to be prepared in a dish or pan, which fits into the stoneware.

Because I use my slow cookers a lot for entertaining, I feel there is a benefit to having two: a smaller (3 to 4 quart) one, which is ideal for preparing dips, roasting nuts or making recipes with smaller yields; and a larger (6 quart) oval one, which is necessary for cooking pot roasts, whole chickens or large quantities of stew-like dishes, as well as for making recipes that call for setting a baking dish or pan inside the stoneware. Once you begin using your slow cooker, you will get a sense of what your own needs are.

Some manufacturers sell a "slow cooker" that is actually a multi-cooker. It has a heating element at the bottom and, in my experience, it cooks faster than a traditional slow cooker. Also, since the heat source is at the bottom, it is possible that the food will scorch during the long cooking time unless it is stirred.

Your slow cooker should come with a booklet that explains how to use the appliance. I recommend that you read this carefully and/or visit the manufacturer's web site for specific information on the model you purchased. I've cooked with a variety of slow cookers and have found that cooking times can vary substantially from one to another. Although it may not seem particularly helpful if you're just starting out, the only firm advice I can give is: Know your slow cooker. After trying a few of these recipes, you will get a sense of whether your slow cooker is faster or slower than the ones I use, and you will be able to adjust the cooking times accordingly.

Other variables that can affect cooking time are extreme humidity, power fluctuations and high altitudes. Be extra vigilant if any of these circumstances affects you.

Cooking Great-Tasting Food

The slow cooker's less-is-better approach is, in many ways, the secret of its success. The appliance does its work by cooking foods very slowly — from about 200°F (90°C) on the **Low** setting to 300°F (150°C) on **High**. This slow, moist cooking environment (remember the tight-fitting lid) enables the appliance to produce mouth-watering pot roasts, briskets, chilies and many other kinds of soups and stews. It also helps to ensure success with delicate puddings and custards, among other dishes. In fact, I'm so pleased with the slow cooker's strengths that there are many dishes I wouldn't cook any other way: for instance, pot roast, beef brisket or short ribs, chilies and many kinds of stew. I also love to make cheesecakes in my slow cooker, as they emerge from this damp cocoon perfectly cooked every time. They don't dry out or crack, which happens all too easily in the oven.

Some Benefits of Long, Slow Cooking
- Breaks down the tough connective tissue of less tender cuts of meat.
- Allows the seasoning in complex sauces to mingle without scorching.
- Makes succulent chilies and stews that don't dry out or stick to the bottom of the pot.
- The low, even heat helps to ensure success with delicate dishes such as puddings and custards.

Slow Cooker Tips

Understanding Your Slow Cooker

Like all appliances, the slow cooker has its unique way of doing things and, as a result, you need to understand how it works and adapt your cooking style accordingly. When friends learned I was writing a slow cooker cookbook, many had a similar response: "Oh, you mean that appliance that allows you to throw the ingredients in and return to a home-cooked meal!"

"Well, sort of," was my response. Over the years, I've learned to think of my slow cooker as an indispensable helpmate and I can hardly imagine living without its assistance. But I also know that it can't work miracles. Off the top of my head, I can't think of any great dish that results when ingredients are merely "thrown together." Success in the slow cooker, like success in the oven or on top of the stove, depends upon using proper cooking techniques. The slow cooker saves you time because it allows you to forget about the food once it is in the stoneware. But you still must pay attention to the advance preparation. Here are a few tips that will help to ensure slow cooker success.

Brown Meat and Soften Vegetables

Although it requires using an extra pan, I am committed to browning meats and softening vegetables before adding them to the slow cooker. In my experience, this is not the most time-consuming part of preparing a slow cooker dish — it usually takes longer to peel and chop the vegetables, which you have to do anyway. But it dramatically improves the quality of the dish for two reasons: not only does browning add color, it begins the process of caramelization, which breaks down the natural sugars in foods and releases their flavor; it also extracts the fat-soluble components of foods, which further enriches the taste. Moreover, tossing herbs and spices with the softened vegetables emulsifies their flavor, helping to produce a sauce in which the flavors are better integrated than they would have been if this step had been skipped.

In the end, I think, this also saves time. After browning, softening and emulsifying the seasonings, I usually add a flour thickener and cook it briefly. Then I stir in liquid that thickens

into gravy during the long, slow cooking. Although these steps take a few minutes at the front end of a recipe, I believe they balance out overall. Once the dish is cooked, there is usually no need to reduce and/or thicken the cooking liquid. Most of the recipes in this book can be served directly from the slow cooker, if desired.

Reduce and Concentrate Liquid
As you use your slow cooker, one of the first things you will notice is that it generates a tremendous amount of liquid. Because slow cookers cook at a low heat, tightly covered, liquid doesn't evaporate as it does in the oven or on top of the stove. As a result, food made from traditional recipes will be watery. So the second rule of successful slow cooking is to reduce the amount of liquid. Naturally, you don't want to reduce the flavor, so I suggest using concentrated broth, usually undiluted. The liquid generated as the dish cooks will thin the broth to its expected strength.

Cut Root Vegetables into Thin Slices or Small Pieces
Perhaps surprisingly, root vegetables — carrots, turnips and, particularly, potatoes — cook even more slowly than meat in the slow cooker. As a result, root vegetables should be thinly sliced or cut into small pieces no larger than 1-inch (2.5 cm) cubes. I have found the mandoline, a device for cutting fruits and vegetables, to be particularly useful for producing the thinly sliced potatoes called for in some recipes.

Pay Attention to Cooking Temperature
To achieve maximum results, less tender cuts of meat should be cooked as slowly as possible at the **Low** setting. Expect to cook whole cuts of meat such as roasts for 10 hours on **Low**, and give brisket 12 hours on **Low** to become truly succulent. If you're short of time and at home during the day, cook whole cuts of meat and whole chicken on **High** for 1 to 2 hours before switching the temperature to **Low**. As noted in Ensuring Food Safety (see page 17), if adding cold ingredients, particularly large cuts of meat, to the slow cooker, set on **High** for 2 hours before lowering the temperature.

Many desserts, such as those containing milk, cream or some leavening agents, need to be cooked on **High**. In these recipes, a **Low** setting is not suggested as an option. For recipes that aren't dependent upon cooking at a particular temperature, the rule of thumb is that 1 hour of cooking on **High** equals 2 to $2\frac{1}{2}$ hours on **Low**.

Don't Overcook

Although slow cooking reduces your chances of overcooking food, it is still not a "one size fits all" solution to meal preparation. If you want your slow cooker to cook while you are away, you should plan your day carefully if you have pork chops or chicken in the pot. Loin pork chops are usually cooked in 5 hours on **Low**. It is very easy to overcook poultry, particularly chicken breasts, in the slow cooker, and unless you are cooking a whole chicken, poultry shouldn't require more than 6 hours on **Low**. If cooking white meat, which dries out easily, I recommend leaving the skin on, which helps to maintain precious moisture and flavor. Remove the skin when serving, if desired. Because legs and thighs stand up well in the slow cooker, I remove the skin before cooking to reduce the fat content in the sauce.

Use Ingredients Appropriately

Some ingredients do not respond well to long, slow cooking and should be added during the last 30 minutes of cooking, after the temperature has been increased to **High**. These include zucchini, peas, snow peas, fish, seafood, milk and cream (which will curdle if cooked too long.)

I love to cook with peppers, but I've learned that most peppers become bitter if cooked for too long. The same holds true for cayenne pepper or hot pepper sauces such as Tabasco, and large quantities of spicy curry powder. (Small quantities of mild curry powder seem to fare well.) The solution to this problem is to add fresh green or red bell peppers to recipes during the last 30 minutes of cooking, use cayenne pepper in small quantities, if at all, and add hot pepper sauce after the dish is cooked. I have also found that several varieties of dried peppers, such as New Mexico or ancho chilies, which become bitter if added to the slow cooker when dry or not fully rehydrated, work well if they are thoroughly soaked in boiling water for 30 minutes before being added to slow cooker recipes. All the recipes in this book address these concerns in the instructions.

Whole Leaf Herbs and Spices

For best results, use whole, rather than ground, herbs and spices in the slow cooker. Whole spices, such as cumin seeds, and whole leaf herbs, such as dried thyme and oregano leaves, release their flavors slowly throughout the long cooking period, unlike ground spices and herbs, which tend to lose flavor during slow cooking. If you're using fresh herbs, add them finely chopped during the last hour of cooking unless you include the whole stem (this works best with thyme and rosemary).

I recommend the use of cracked black peppercorns rather than ground pepper in many of my recipes because they release flavor slowly during the long cooking process. "Cracked pepper" can be purchased in the spice sections of supermarkets, but I like to make my own in a mortar with a pestle. If you prefer to use ground black pepper, use one-quarter to half the amount of cracked black peppercorns called for in the recipe.

Using Dishes and Pans in the Slow Cooker

Some recipes, notably puddings and custards, need to be cooked in an extra dish placed in the slow cooker stoneware. Not only will you need a large oval slow cooker for this purpose, finding a dish or pan that fits into the stoneware can be a challenge. I've found that standard 7-inch (17.5 cm) square, 4-cup (1 L) and 6-cup (1.5 L) ovenproof baking dishes are the best all-round dishes for this purpose, and I've used them to cook most of the custard-like recipes in this book. A 7-inch (17.5 cm) springform pan, which fits into a large oval slow cooker, is also a useful purchase for making cheesecakes and other desserts.

Before you decide to make a recipe requiring a baking dish, ensure that you have a container that will fit into your stoneware. I've noted the size and dimensions of the containers used in all relevant recipes. Be aware that varying the size and shape of the dish is likely to affect cooking times.

Maximize Slow Cooker Convenience

Although slow cookers can produce mouth-watering food, the appliance's other great strength is convenience. Where appropriate, all my recipes contain a make-ahead tip to help you maximize this attribute. To get the most out of your slow cooker, consider the following:
- Prepare ingredients to the cooking stage the night before you intend to cook, to keep work to a minimum in the morning.
- Cook a recipe overnight and refrigerate until ready to serve.

Ensuring Food Safety

Slow cooker manufacturers have designed the appliance to ensure that bacterial growth is not a concern. According to the U.S. Department of Agriculture, bacteria in food is killed at a temperature of 165°F (74°C). As long as the lid is left on and the food is cooked for the appropriate length of time, that temperature will be reached quickly enough to ensure food safety. Most of the ingredients in my recipes are warm when added to the slow cooker (the meat has been browned and the sauce thickened on the stovetop), which adds a cushion of comfort to any potential concerns about food safety.

The following tips will help to ensure that utmost food safety standards are met:

- Do not allow ingredients to come to room temperature before cooking.
- Do not refrigerate uncooked meat or poultry in the slow cooker stoneware as the insert will become very cold, which will slow the cooking process.
- Do not partially cook meat or poultry and refrigerate for subsequent cooking.
- If preparing ingredients in advance of cooking, refrigerate in separate containers and assemble when ready to cook.
- Pay attention to the make-ahead instructions for those recipes that can be partially prepared in advance of cooking, as they have been developed to address food safety issues.
- If cooking a large cut of meat, such as a pot roast, which has been added to the stoneware without being browned, set the temperature at **High** for 2 hours to accelerate the cooking process. Then reduce to **Low** for the duration of the cooking time.
- Thaw frozen food before adding to the slow cooker. Adding it in a frozen state will increase the time required for the temperature to reach the "safe zone," where bacteria growth is inhibited. Frozen fruits and vegetables should be thawed under cold running water to separate before being added to recipes.
- When cooking whole poultry, which requires a longer cooking time in order for a safe temperature to reach the bone, test doneness by inserting an instant-read thermometer inside the thickest part of the thigh to ensure that the temperature has reached 170°F (80°C).
- Don't lift the lid while food is cooking. Each time the lid is removed, it takes approximately 20 minutes to recover the lost heat. This increases the time it takes for the food to reach the "safe zone."
- Refrigerate leftovers as quickly as possible.
- Do not reheat food in the slow cooker.

Dips, Starters and Snacks

Mushroom and Roasted Garlic Crostini

Mushroom and Roasted Garlic Crostini

MAKES ENOUGH FOR 28 CROSTINI

Everyone loves this tasty all-purpose hors d'oeuvre, which is both simple and elegant. It can be used as the first course to a dinner or as a party canapé.

• *Works best in a small (maximum 3½ quart) slow cooker*

8	cloves roasted garlic (see Tips, below)	8
1 lb	white mushrooms, cleaned and trimmed (see Tips, below)	500 g
2	large French shallots, finely chopped	2
2 tbsp	extra-virgin olive oil	25 mL
¼ cup	dry white wine or dry white vermouth	50 mL
2 tbsp	chopped fresh parsley leaves	25 mL
2 tbsp	whipping cream, optional	25 mL
2 tsp	balsamic vinegar	10 mL
	Salt and freshly ground black pepper	
28	crostini (see Tips, below)	28
	Crumbled soft goat cheese	

1. In slow cooker stoneware, combine garlic, mushrooms, shallots, olive oil and wine. Cover and cook on **Low** for 8 hours or on **High** for 4 hours, until mushrooms are soft. Drain off liquid (see Tip, below).

2. Place mushroom mixture in a food processor with parsley and pulse until ingredients are very finely chopped but not puréed. Add whipping cream, if using, vinegar, salt and black pepper to taste and pulse two or three times to combine.

3. Preheat oven to 375°F (190°C). Spread mushroom mixture over crostini. Sprinkle goat cheese on top. Place on baking sheet and bake until cheese begins to brown and melt. Serve hot.

TIPS

• An easy way to roast this quantity of garlic is to peel the cloves, remove the pith (the center part that often sprouts), then place the cloves on a piece of foil. Drizzle about ½ tsp (2 mL) olive oil over the garlic, then fold up the foil to make a tight packet. Bake in 400°F (200°C) oven for 20 minutes.

• Leave small mushrooms whole. Cut larger ones into halves or quarters.

• Keep a bottle of dry white vermouth on hand as it makes a satisfactory substitute for dry white wine. That way, you don't have to open a bottle of wine when you need only a small quantity.

• Cover and refrigerate the mushroom cooking liquid. It is a great addition to soups, stews and gravies, along with or instead of broth.

• To make crostini: Preheat broiler. Brush baguette slices on both sides with olive oil and toast under broiler, turning once.

Chili con Queso

**MAKES ABOUT
4 CUPS (1 L)**
....

This delicious combination of hot peppers, tomatoes, corn and melted cheese includes versatility as part of its charm. Team it up with tortilla chips or crudités for a great dip. For a light lunch, spread on a warm tortilla, roll up and garnish with chopped green or red onions and sour cream.

• *Works best in a small (maximum 3½ quart) slow cooker*

1 tbsp	vegetable oil	15 mL
2	onions, finely chopped	2
4	cloves garlic, minced	4
1 to 2	jalapeño peppers, minced	1 to 2
2 tsp	chili powder	10 mL
1 tsp	dried oregano leaves	5 mL
1 tsp	cracked black peppercorns	5 mL
1 tsp	salt	5 mL
2	tomatoes, peeled and diced	2
1 cup	corn kernels, thawed if frozen	250 mL
2 cups	shredded Monterey Jack or Cheddar cheese	500 mL
¼ cup	sour cream	50 mL
1	roasted red bell pepper, chopped, optional (see Tips, page 24)	1

1. In a skillet, heat oil over medium heat. Add onions and cook until softened. Add garlic, jalapeño pepper, chili powder, oregano, peppercorns and salt and cook, stirring, for 1 minute. Stir in tomatoes and corn and cook until mixture is bubbling. Transfer to slow cooker stoneware.

2. Add cheese, sour cream and red pepper, if using. Stir well. Cover and cook on **High** for 1½ hours, until hot and bubbling.
....

TIP
• If you don't have time to roast a pepper, use good-quality bottled roasted peppers.

PANTRY NOTES
....

Jalapeño Peppers
Probably the most common chili in North America, medium-hot jalapeños are the basis for many dishes with a Tex-Mex or South American flavor. They are usually available in the produce section of supermarkets. In my opinion, their unique flavor limits their use mainly to dishes inspired by North and South American cuisine.

Black Bean and Salsa Dip

**MAKES ABOUT
3 CUPS (750 ML)**

*This tasty
Cuban-inspired dip
can be made from
ingredients you're
likely to have on
hand. Nutritious and
flavorful, it's a welcome
treat, anytime of the
day. Serve with tortilla
chips, tostadas, crisp
crackers or crudités.*

• *Works best in a small (maximum 3½ quart) slow cooker*

1	can (19 oz/540 mL) black beans, drained and rinsed or 1 cup (250 mL) dried black beans, cooked and drained (see Basic Beans, page 214)	1
8 oz	cream cheese, cubed	250 g
½ cup	tomato salsa	125 mL
¼ cup	sour cream	50 mL
1 tsp	chili powder	5 mL
1 tsp	cumin seeds	5 mL
1 tsp	cracked black peppercorns	5 mL
1	jalapeño pepper, finely chopped (see Tips, below), optional	1
1	roasted red bell pepper, finely chopped, optional (see Tips, below)	1
	Finely chopped green onion, optional	
	Finely chopped cilantro, optional	

1. In slow cooker stoneware, combine ingredients, except for green onion or cilantro, if using. Cover and cook on **High** for 1 hour. Stir again and cook on **High** for an additional 30 minutes, until mixture is hot and bubbly. Serve immediately or set temperature at **Low** until ready to serve. Garnish with green onion and/or cilantro, if desired.

TIPS

• For a smoother dip, purée the beans in a food processor or mash with a potato masher before adding to stoneware.

• If you use a five-alarm salsa in this dip, you may find it too spicy with the addition of jalapeño pepper.

• If you don't have time to roast your own pepper, use a bottled roasted red pepper.

• To roast peppers: Preheat oven to 400°F (200°C). Place pepper(s) on a baking sheet and roast, turning two or three times, until the skin on all sides is blackened. (This will take about 25 minutes.) Transfer pepper(s) to a heatproof bowl. Cover with a plate and let stand until cool. Remove and, using a sharp knife, lift off skins. Discard skins and slice according to recipe instructions.

Ball Park Bean Dip

**MAKES ABOUT
4 CUPS (1 L)**

*The processed cheese
in this dip brings
back memories of my
childhood. As the runny
center of a grilled cheese
sandwich made with
doughy white bread or
spread on celery sticks for
an after-school snack,
processed cheese was
the ultimate comfort
food. Today, as the
key ingredient in the
dripping nachos served
at baseball games, its
retro overtones enhance
the ballpark ambience.
Enjoy this dip while
watching televised
sports events and any
other time you crave
its particular charms.
Serve with celery sticks
or tortilla or corn
chips and watch it
quickly disappear.*

• *Works best in a small (maximum 3$\frac{1}{2}$ quart) slow cooker*

6	green onions, white part only, finely chopped	6
1	can (14 oz/398 mL) refried beans (see Tip, below)	1
1	package (16 oz/500 g) processed cheese, cut into $\frac{1}{2}$-inch (1 cm) cubes	1
$\frac{1}{2}$ cup	tomato salsa	125 mL
2	cloves garlic, minced	2
1	jalapeño pepper, finely chopped	1
2 tsp	chili powder	10 mL
$\frac{1}{4}$ tsp	freshly ground black pepper	1 mL

1. In slow cooker stoneware, combine ingredients. Cover and cook on **Low** for 4 hours or on **High** for 2 hours, until cheese is melted and mixture is bubbling. Stir well and serve.

TIP

• Refried beans are cooked beans that are then fried — they are not fried twice, as their name suggests. If you don't have a can of refried beans in the pantry, you can easily make your own for use in this recipe. Drain and rinse 1 can (19 oz/540 mL) pinto, kidney or black beans. Using a fork or potato masher, mash until chunky. (You can also do this in a food processor.) In a skillet, heat 1 tbsp (15 mL) vegetable oil over medium heat. (If you want to be authentically Mexican, use lard instead.) Add beans and cook, stirring, for about 5 minutes, until they have thickened and resemble a chunky potato mash.

Spicy Artichoke Dip

**MAKES ABOUT
3 CUPS (750 ML)**

This creamy dip, with an intriguing hint of spice, is flavorful and light if made with lower-fat cheeses and mayonnaise. Serve with tostadas, tortilla or pita chips.

• *Works best in a small (maximum 3$\frac{1}{2}$ quart) slow cooker*

1 tbsp	chili powder (see Tip, below)	15 mL
1	can (14 oz/398 mL) artichokes, drained and chopped	1
8 oz	light cream cheese, cubed	250 g
$\frac{1}{2}$ cup	shredded lower-fat mozzarella cheese	125 mL
4	green onions, white part only, finely chopped	4
1	clove garlic, minced	1
1	jalapeño pepper, minced	1
2 tbsp	light mayonnaise	25 mL
1 tbsp	Dijon mustard	15 mL
1 tsp	Worcestershire sauce	5 mL
$\frac{1}{2}$ tsp	salt	2 mL
$\frac{1}{4}$ tsp	freshly ground black pepper	1 mL

1. In slow cooker stoneware, combine ingredients. Cover and cook on **High** for 2 hours, until hot and bubbling. Stir well and serve.

TIP
• Although packaged chili powder works well in this recipe, I prefer to make this dip with ancho or New Mexico chili powder, both of which are available in many supermarkets or specialty stores. If you have a spice grinder, you can make your own by grinding dried chili peppers of the preferred variety. (You will need about 1 dried pepper to make the appropriate quantity of chili powder.) Or, you can soak 1 dried ancho or New Mexico chili pepper for 30 minutes in boiling water; remove the stem, chop finely and add to the mixture instead of the chili powder.

Nippy Oyster and Bacon Dip

**MAKES ABOUT
2 CUPS (500 ML)**

....

*When it is cold outside,
there is nothing more
satisfying than a hot
and bubbling dip loaded
with flavor. One
advantage to this rich,
creamy infusion is its
versatility. For an
impressive presentation,
spoon into a serving
bowl and surround
with a big platter of
vegetables for dipping,
such as blanched
broccoli, cauliflower or
Brussels sprouts and
crispy potato wedges.
If simplicity is the order
of the day, open a bag
of potato chips. Either
way, this dip always
earns rave reviews.*

• *Works best in a small (maximum 3½ quart) slow cooker*

2	slices bacon, cooked to crisp, then crumbled	2
8 oz	cream cheese, softened	250 g
1 cup	shredded Cheddar cheese, preferably old	250 mL
2 tbsp	mayonnaise	25 mL
¼ tsp	freshly ground black pepper	1 mL
½ to 1	jalapeño pepper, seeded and finely chopped	½ to 1
1	can (4 oz/85 g) smoked oysters, drained and cut in half	1
1	roasted red bell pepper, finely chopped (see Tips, page 24)	1
	Potato chips, optional	
	Crispy Potato Wedges (see Tip, below), optional	
	Brussels sprouts, cooked until slightly underdone, optional	
	Blanched broccoli spears or cauliflower florets, optional	

1. In slow cooker stoneware, combine bacon, cream cheese, Cheddar cheese, mayonnaise, black pepper and jalapeño pepper. Stir well. Cover and cook on **High** for 1 hour. Add oysters and red pepper and stir again. Cook on **High** for an additional 30 minutes, until hot and bubbly. Serve immediately or set temperature at **Low** until ready to serve.

....

TIP

• To make Crispy Potato Wedges: Bake the desired number of baking potatoes in a 400°F (200°C) oven for 1 hour. Set aside to cool. Thirty minutes before serving the dip, cut each potato into 8 wedges. Brush with olive oil, place in 400°F (200°C) oven and roast until crisp and golden.

....

VARIATION

Nippy Clam and Bacon Dip: Substitute 1 can (5 oz/142 g) drained clams for the smoked oysters. Add along with the bacon.

Cheese Loaves with Mushroom Tomato Sauce

SERVES 6 AS A STARTER OR 4 AS A LIGHT MEAL

This is a versatile and delicious dish. Serve it as a starter to an elegant meal or as the centerpiece of a light dinner or lunch. If using canned tomatoes, use good-quality Italian tomatoes, such as San Marzano, for the sauce.

• *2 mini loaf pans (6 by 3 inches/15 by 7.5 cm), lightly greased*

Cheese Loaves

2 cups	table (18%) cream	500 mL
2	eggs	2
2	egg yolks	2
½ tsp	paprika	2 mL
½ tsp	salt	2 mL
¼ tsp	freshly ground black pepper	1 mL
¾ cup	freshly grated Parmesan cheese	175 mL

Mushroom Tomato Sauce

2 tbsp	butter	25 mL
8 oz	cremini mushrooms, sliced	250 g
½ tsp	salt	2 mL
¼ tsp	freshly ground black pepper	1 mL
¼ tsp	dried oregano leaves	1 mL
4	green onions, white part only, finely chopped	4
2 cups	tomatoes, peeled and diced or 1 can (28 oz/796 mL) tomatoes, drained and chopped	500 mL

1. Cheese Loaves: In a bowl, whisk cream with eggs and egg yolks until well integrated. Whisk in paprika, salt and black pepper. Stir in cheese. Divide mixture equally between prepared pans. Cover with foil and tie with string. Place in slow cooker stoneware and pour in enough boiling water to come 1 inch (2.5 cm) up the sides. Cover and cook on **High** for 3 hours or until a knife inserted in loaf comes out clean.

2. Mushroom Tomato Sauce: In a skillet, melt butter over medium heat. Add mushrooms and cook, stirring, until they release their liquid. Add salt, black pepper and oregano and cook, stirring, for 1 minute. Add onions and tomatoes and cook, stirring frequently, until sauce thickens.

3. When ready to serve, remove foil from loaf pans, run a sharp knife around the loaves and invert onto a large platter. Spoon Mushroom Tomato Sauce over loaves and serve immediately.

TIP
• Many supermarkets stock mini loaf pans among their selection of foil baking pans.

Peppercorn Pâté

*This flavorful pâté
makes a delicious lunch
or an excellent hors
d'oeuvre. Serve with the
same accompaniments
and condiments listed
for the Country Terrine
with Pistachios (see
recipe, page 32).*

- *Loaf pan, earthenware terrine or soufflé dish (see Tips, page 33)*
- *Large (minimum 5 quart) oval slow cooker*

1 lb	lean ground pork	500 g
1 lb	lean ground veal	500 g
¼ cup	white wine or dry white vermouth	50 mL
2 tbsp	brandy or cognac	25 mL
2 tbsp	butter	25 mL
1	leek, white part only, cleaned and finely chopped	1
2 tsp	cracked black peppercorns	10 mL
1 tsp	salt	5 mL
½ tsp	dried thyme leaves	2 mL
1	egg	1
1 tbsp	all-purpose flour	15 mL
4	slices bacon	4

1. In a mixing bowl, combine pork, veal, wine and brandy. Mix well and set aside.

2. In a skillet, melt butter over medium heat. Add leek and cook until softened. Add peppercorns, salt and thyme and cook, stirring, for 1 minute. Add to meat mixture.

3. In a bowl, whisk egg with flour until smooth. Add to meat mixture and mix until ingredients are well combined.

4. Lay 2 strips of bacon on the bottom of the baking dish. Spread mixture evenly over top. Lay remaining bacon over top. Cover pan tightly with foil and secure with string. Place pan in slow cooker stoneware and pour in enough boiling water to come 1 inch (2.5 cm) up the sides. Cover and cook on **High** for 4 hours or until interior temperature reaches 170°F (80°C).

5. Remove terrine from slow cooker stoneware. Do not remove foil. Place a brick or other heavy item that fits into the pan on top and refrigerate overnight or longer to allow the flavors to develop. (Pâté will keep refrigerated for up to three days.) To unmold, dip the pan in hot water. Run a sharp knife around the inside of the dish, then invert the terrine onto a serving plate. Scrape away and discard the accumulated fat. To serve, slice thinly.

Country Terrine with Pistachios

**MAKES ABOUT
2½ LBS (1.25 KG)**

This country-style terrine, which is really just a spiffy cold meat loaf, is versatile and easy to make. For a traditional French-style lunch, serve with salad, crusty bread, good mustard and pickles. Finish with fresh fruit and cheese. Or pack everything up in a cooler and enjoy a memorable picnic. It also makes an excellent hors d'oeuvre served on slices of fresh baguette spread with Dijon mustard.

- *Loaf pan, earthenware terrine or soufflé dish (see Tips, right)*
- *Large (minimum 5 quart) oval slow cooker*

3 oz	pancetta (see Tips, right)	90 g
2	onions, quartered	2
1	clove garlic, chopped	1
1 lb	ground veal	500 g
1 lb	ground pork	500 g
2 tbsp	dry sherry	25 mL
½ cup	ground pistachios (about 2 oz/60 g shelled pistachio nuts)	125 mL
1 tsp	cracked black peppercorns	5 mL
1 tsp	salt	5 mL
1 tsp	dried thyme leaves	5 mL
¼ tsp	ground allspice	1 mL
4	bay leaves	4

1. In a food processor, combine pancetta, onions and garlic. Process until onions and pancetta are finely chopped.

2. In a bowl, combine pancetta mixture, veal, pork, sherry, pistachios, peppercorns, salt, thyme and allspice. Using your hands, mix until ingredients are well blended.

3. Lay bay leaves evenly across bottom of terrine. Spread mixture evenly over top. Cover tightly with foil and secure with string. Place pan in slow cooker stoneware and pour in enough boiling water to come 1 inch (2.5 cm) up the sides. Cover and cook on **Low** for 6 hours or on **High** for 3 hours or until interior temperature reaches 170°F (80°C).

4. Remove terrine from slow cooker stoneware. Do not remove foil. Place a brick or other heavy item that fits into the pan on top and refrigerate overnight or longer to allow the flavors to develop. (Pâté will keep refrigerated for up to three days.)

5. To unmold, dip the pan in hot water. Run a sharp knife around the inside of the dish, then invert the terrine onto a serving plate. Scrape away and discard the accumulated fat. To serve, slice thinly.

TIPS

• Pancetta is Italian cured bacon and is available in most supermarkets or in specialty food stores. If you can't find it, use a smoked ham, such as Black Forest ham, instead.

• This terrine can be made in almost any kind of baking dish that will fit into your slow cooker. I have a variety of baking pans that work well: a small loaf pan (approximately 8 by 5 inches/20 by 12.5 cm) makes a traditionally shaped terrine; a round (4-cup/1 L) soufflé dish or a square (7-inch/17.5 cm) baking dish produces slices of different shapes.

Crab Supreme

**MAKES ABOUT
2 CUPS (500 ML)**

....

This is great starter for even the most elegant meal. Spread on crackers, toast points, crostini or Belgian endive spears. Open some cold white wine and wait for the compliments.

• *Works best in a small (maximum 3½ quart) slow cooker*

2	cans (each 6 oz/170 g) cooked crabmeat, drained and chopped	2
6 oz	cream cheese, softened	175 g
¼ cup	finely chopped red bell pepper	50 mL
¼ cup	finely chopped green onion	50 mL
2 tbsp	finely chopped fresh parsley	25 mL
2 tbsp	mayonnaise	25 mL
1 tbsp	Dijon mustard	15 mL
1 tsp	Worcestershire sauce	5 mL
¼ tsp	salt	1 mL
¼ tsp	freshly ground black pepper	1 mL
2 tbsp	capers, drained and minced	25 mL
Dash	hot pepper sauce	Dash
	Paprika	

1. In slow cooker stoneware, combine crabmeat, cream cheese, bell pepper, green onion, parsley, mayonnaise, Dijon mustard, Worcestershire sauce, salt and black pepper. Cover and cook on **High** for 1 hour. Stir in capers and hot pepper sauce. Cover and cook for 30 minutes, until mixture is hot and bubbly. To serve, spread on crackers and dust lightly with paprika.

Hot Roasted Nuts

**MAKES 2 CUPS
(500 ML)**

....

*Use your slow cooker
to make your own
better-than-store-bought
version of tasty
tamari-roasted almonds.*

• These recipes work best in a small (maximum 3½ quart) slow cooker

Chinese Almonds

2 cups	unblanched almonds	500 mL
¼ tsp	freshly ground black pepper	1 mL
2 tbsp	tamari or soy sauce	25 mL
1 tbsp	extra-virgin olive oil	15 mL
1 tsp	fine sea salt	5 mL
½ tsp	granulated sugar	2 mL

1. In slow cooker stoneware, combine almonds and black pepper. Cover and cook on **High** for 1½ hours, stirring every 30 minutes, until nuts are nicely toasted.

2. In a bowl, combine remaining ingredients. Add to hot almonds in slow cooker stoneware and stir thoroughly to combine. Spoon mixture into a small serving bowl and serve hot or allow to cool.

*Everyone loves these hot
buttery peanuts — even
me, and I'm usually not
a fan of this Southern
legume. Use peanuts
with skins on or buy
them peeled, depending
upon your preference.
Both work well in
this recipe.*

Buttery Peanuts

2 cups	raw peanuts	500 mL
¼ cup	melted butter	50 mL
2 tsp	fine sea salt	10 mL

1. In slow cooker stoneware, combine peanuts and butter. Cover and cook on **High** for 2 to 2½ hours, stirring occasionally, until peanuts are nicely roasted. Drain on paper towels. Place in a bowl, sprinkle with salt and stir to combine.

....

VARIATION
Curried Buttery Peanuts: In a small bowl, combine salt with 2 tsp (10 mL) curry powder and pinch cayenne pepper. Sprinkle hot peanuts with this mixture instead of plain salt and stir to combine.

If your taste buds are down in the dumps, grab their attention with a batch of these spicy nibblers. They are great with a long, cold beer.

Curried Almonds

2 cups	unblanched almonds	500 mL
¼ tsp	freshly ground white pepper	1 mL
2 tbsp	melted butter	25 mL
1 tbsp	Worcestershire sauce	15 mL
1 tsp	curry powder	5 mL
1 tsp	fine sea salt	5 mL

1. In slow cooker stoneware, combine almonds and white pepper. Cover and cook on **High** for 1½ hours, stirring every 30 minutes, until nuts are nicely toasted.

2. In a bowl, combine remaining ingredients. Add to hot almonds in slow cooker stoneware and stir thoroughly to combine. Spoon mixture into a small serving bowl and serve hot or allow to cool.

If you like nuts with a sweet finish, try these delicious pecans. Don't expect leftovers, as they are very popular.

Orange-Spiced Pecans

2 cups	pecan halves	500 mL
2 tbsp	orange juice	25 mL
¼ cup	granulated sugar	50 mL
1 tbsp	grated orange zest	15 mL
½ tsp	ground cinnamon	2 mL
¼ tsp	freshly grated nutmeg	1 mL
Pinch	fine sea salt	Pinch

1. In slow cooker stoneware, combine pecans and orange juice. Cover and cook on **High** for 1 hour or until nuts release their aroma and are nicely toasted. Transfer to a serving bowl.

2. In a small bowl, combine sugar, orange zest, cinnamon, nutmeg and salt. Pour over hot nuts and toss to combine. Serve warm.

TIP
• Nuts tend to burn easily because of their high fat content. Watch carefully once they start to release their aroma as they are close to being done.

Soups

Red Lentil and Carrot Soup with Coconut

Red Lentil and Carrot Soup with Coconut

SERVES 8 TO 10 AS A STARTER OR 4 TO 6 AS A MAIN COURSE

I love the combination of flavors in this unusual soup. The red lentils partially dissolve while cooking, creating a creamy texture without adding fat. The carrots enhance color as well as taste, and the coconut milk creates an intriguing, almost nutty note. The combination is mouth-watering. Serve as a starter or add an Indian bread such as naan, and a green salad for a delicious light meal.

MAKE AHEAD
This soup can be partially prepared the night before it is cooked, but without adding the coconut milk. Complete Steps 1 and 2. Cover and refrigerate overnight. The next day, continue cooking as directed in Step 3.

2 cups	red lentils	500 mL
1 tbsp	vegetable oil	15 mL
2	onions, finely chopped	2
4	cloves garlic, minced	4
2 tsp	turmeric	10 mL
2 tsp	cumin seeds	10 mL
1 tsp	salt	5 mL
½ tsp	cracked black peppercorns	2mL
1	long red chili pepper or 2 Thai chilies, finely chopped (see Tip, below)	1
1	can (28 oz/796 mL) tomatoes, including juice	1
2	large carrots, peeled, cut in half lengthwise and thinly sliced	2
1 tbsp	freshly squeezed lemon juice	15 mL
6 cups	vegetable or chicken broth	1.5 L
1	can (14 oz/398 mL) coconut milk	1
	Thin slices lemon, optional	
	Finely chopped cilantro, optional	

1. In a colander, rinse lentils thoroughly under cold running water. Set aside.

2. In a skillet, heat oil over medium heat. Add onions and cook, stirring, until soft. Add garlic, turmeric, cumin seeds, salt, peppercorns and chili pepper and cook, stirring, for 1 minute. Add tomatoes and bring to a boil, breaking up with the back of a spoon. Stir in carrots, lentils, lemon juice and broth.

3. Transfer mixture to slow cooker stoneware. Cover and cook on **Low** for 8 to 10 hours or on **High** for 4 to 5 hours, until carrots are tender and mixture is bubbling. Stir in coconut milk and cook on **High** for 20 to 30 minutes, until heated through.

4. When ready to serve, ladle into bowls and top with lemon slices and cilantro, if using.

TIP
• If you don't have fresh chili peppers, stir in your favorite hot pepper sauce, to taste, just before serving.

Mediterranean Lentil Soup with Spinach

SERVES 6 TO 8

This delicious soup, delicately flavored with lemon and cumin, reminds me of hot, languid days under the Mediterranean sun. Serve it as a starter or add a green salad and warm country-style bread for a refreshing and nutritious light meal.

MAKE AHEAD
This soup can be partially prepared the night before it is cooked, but without adding the spinach and lemon juice. Complete Step 1. Cover and refrigerate overnight. The next day, continue cooking as directed in Step 2.

1 cup	green or brown lentils	250 mL
2	onions, chopped	2
2	stalks celery, peeled and chopped	2
2	large carrots, peeled and chopped	2
1	potato, peeled and grated	1
1	clove garlic, minced	1
1 tsp	cumin seeds	5 mL
1 tsp	grated lemon zest	5 mL
6 cups	vegetable or chicken broth	1.5 L
1 lb	fresh spinach leaves or 1 package (10 oz/300 g) spinach, washed, stems removed and coarsely chopped	500 g
2 tbsp	freshly squeezed lemon juice	25 mL

1. In a colander, rinse lentils thoroughly under cold running water. In slow cooker stoneware, combine lentils, onions, celery, carrots, potato, garlic, cumin seeds, lemon zest and broth.

2. Cover and cook on **Low** for 8 to 10 hours or on **High** for 4 to 6 hours, until vegetables are tender. Add spinach and lemon juice. Cover and cook on **High** for 20 minutes, until spinach is cooked and mixture is hot and bubbly.

Santa Fe Sweet Potato Soup

SERVES 6 TO 8

Here's a flavorful, rib-sticking soup with lots of pizzazz and universal appeal. The enticing, slightly smoky flavor of the New Mexico chilies permeates the broth, and the lime, roasted red pepper and cilantro finish provides a nice balance to the sweet potatoes. If you are a heat seeker, add the jalapeño pepper.

MAKE AHEAD
This soup can be assembled the night before it is cooked. Follow preparation directions in Steps 1 and 2. Cover and refrigerate overnight. The next day, continue cooking as directed in Steps 3 and 4.

2	dried New Mexico chili peppers	2
2 cups	boiling water	500 mL
1 tbsp	vegetable oil	15 mL
2	onions, finely chopped	2
4	cloves garlic, minced	4
1	finely chopped jalapeño pepper, optional (see left)	1
1 tsp	salt	5 mL
1 tsp	dried oregano leaves	5 mL
4 cups	peeled, cubed sweet potatoes, about ½ inch (1 cm)	1 L
6 cups	vegetable or chicken broth	1.5 L
2 cups	corn kernels, thawed if frozen	500 mL
1 tsp	grated lime zest	5 mL
2 tbsp	lime juice	25 mL
2	roasted red peppers, cut into thin strips (see Tips, page 24)	2
	Finely chopped cilantro	

1. In a heatproof bowl, soak chilies in boiling water for 30 minutes. Drain, discarding soaking liquid and stems. Pat dry, chop finely and set aside.

2. In a skillet, heat oil over medium heat. Add onions and cook, stirring, until softened. Add garlic, jalapeño pepper, if using, salt, oregano and reserved chilies and cook, stirring, for 1 minute. Transfer mixture to slow cooker stoneware. Add sweet potatoes and broth and stir to combine.

3. Cover and cook on **Low** for 8 to 10 hours or on **High** for 4 to 6 hours, until sweet potatoes are tender. Strain vegetables, reserving broth. In a blender or food processor, purée vegetables with 1 cup (250 mL) reserved broth until smooth. Return mixture, along with reserved broth, to slow cooker stoneware. Or, using a hand-held blender, purée the soup in stoneware. Add corn, lime zest and juice. Cover and cook on **High** for 20 minutes, until corn is tender.

4. When ready to serve, ladle soup into individual bowls and garnish with red pepper strips and cilantro.

Creamy Corn Chowder

SERVES 6

Here's a comfort food classic that never goes out of style. In addition to adding nutrients and substance to the soup, the potatoes thicken and add flavor to the broth. If you like a bit of spice, add the jalapeño pepper.

MAKE AHEAD
This soup can be partially prepared the night before it is cooked. Complete Steps 1 and 2. Do not add potatoes. Cover and refrigerate overnight. The next morning, stir in potatoes and continue cooking as directed in Step 3.

2	slices bacon	2
2	onions, finely chopped	2
2	stalks celery, peeled and thinly sliced	2
2	carrots, peeled and diced	2
1/2 tsp	poultry seasoning (see Tip, below)	2 mL
1	jalapeño pepper, finely chopped, optional	1
1 tsp	salt	5 mL
1/2 tsp	cracked black peppercorns	2 mL
1	bay leaf	1
3 1/2 cups	vegetable or chicken broth	875 mL
2	large potatoes, peeled and grated	2
2	cans (each 19 oz/540 mL) cream-style corn	2
1	green bell pepper, seeded and finely chopped	1

1. In a skillet, cook bacon over medium-high heat until crisp. Drain thoroughly on paper towel. Crumble and set aside, covered, in refrigerator. Drain all but 1 tbsp (15 mL) fat from pan.

2. Reduce heat to medium. Add onions, celery and carrots to pan and cook, stirring, until softened. Add poultry seasoning, jalapeño pepper, if using, salt, peppercorns and bay leaf and cook, stirring, for 1 minute. Add broth and bring to a boil. Transfer mixture to slow cooker stoneware. Stir in potatoes.

3. Cover and cook on **Low** for 8 hours or on **High** for 4 hours, until vegetables are tender. Add corn, green pepper and reserved bacon. Stir well. Cover and cook on **High** for 30 minutes, until soup is hot and bubbly.

TIP
• If you don't have poultry seasoning, use dried thyme leaves instead.

VARIATIONS
Creamy Corn Chowder with Scallops: In a skillet over medium heat, melt 2 tbsp (25 mL) butter. Add 8 oz (250 g) scallops, lightly seasoned with salt and freshly ground black pepper and cook, stirring, until scallops are browned on both sides and cooked through, about 2 minutes. Add to hot soup just before serving.
Smoked Salmon and Corn Chowder: Add chopped smoked salmon, to taste, to hot chowder just before serving.

Cumin-Flavored Black Bean Soup with Tomato

SERVES 6 TO 8

I love the in-your-face flavors of this robust, Latin American-inspired soup and can rarely resist a second helping. For an eye-catching presentation, ladle the soup into earthenware bowls, add a heaping spoonful of chopped avocado, top with a dollop of sour cream and garnish with cilantro. It looks every bit as good as it tastes.

MAKE AHEAD
This dish can be assembled the night before it is cooked. Complete Steps 1 and 2. Cover and refrigerate overnight. The next morning, continue cooking as directed in Step 3.

2 tbsp	cumin seeds	25 mL
1 tbsp	vegetable oil	15 mL
2	onions, finely chopped	2
4	cloves garlic, minced	4
1	jalapeño pepper, finely chopped	1
1 tsp	salt	5 mL
½ tsp	cracked black peppercorns	2 mL
1	can (28 oz/796 mL) tomatoes, including juice, coarsely chopped	1
6 cups	vegetable or chicken broth	1.5 L
2	cans (each 19 oz/540 mL) black beans, drained and rinsed, or 2 cups (500 mL) dried black beans, soaked and cooked (see Basic Beans, page 214)	2
2 tbsp	freshly squeezed lemon juice	25 mL
	Sour cream	
	Finely chopped cilantro, optional	
	Finely chopped green onion, optional	
	Chopped avocado, optional	

1. In a dry skillet, toast cumin seeds over medium heat until lightly browned and aroma is released. Immediately transfer to a small bowl. When cool, grind seeds in a spice grinder, with a rolling pin or in a mortar with a pestle. Set aside.

2. In a skillet, heat oil over medium heat. Add onions and cook, stirring, until softened. Add garlic, jalapeño pepper, salt, peppercorns and reserved cumin and cook, stirring, for 1 minute. Add tomatoes and bring to a boil. Transfer mixture to slow cooker stoneware. Add broth and beans and stir well.

3. Cover and cook on **Low** for 8 to 10 hours or on **High** for 4 to 6 hours. Stir in lemon juice. In a blender or food processor, purée soup in batches. Or, using a hand-held blender, purée the soup in stoneware.

4. When ready to serve, ladle soup into bowls, add a dollop of sour cream and garnish with cilantro, green onion and avocados, as desired.

Tortilla Soup with Corn and Chilies

This is my husband's favorite soup. He can't get enough of the smoky broth and the creamy avocados, which make an irresistible combination.

MAKE AHEAD
This soup can be partially prepared the night before it is cooked. Complete Steps 1 through 3. Cover and refrigerate overnight. The next morning, continue cooking as directed.

1	dried New Mexico chili pepper	1
2 cups	boiling water	500 mL
2	slices bacon	2
2	onions, finely chopped	2
2	cloves garlic, minced	2
1 tbsp	cumin seeds	15 mL
1 tbsp	dried oregano leaves	15 mL
1 tsp	grated lime zest	5 mL
1 tsp	salt	5 mL
$\frac{1}{2}$ tsp	cracked black peppercorns	2 mL
1	can (19 oz/540 mL) pinto beans, drained and rinsed, or 1 cup (250 mL) dried pinto beans, soaked, cooked and drained (see Basic Beans, page 214)	1
1	can (28 oz/796 mL) tomatoes, including juice	1
6 cups	vegetable or chicken broth	1.5 L
1	can (4.5 oz/127 mL) mild green chilies, drained	1
2 cups	corn kernels	500 mL
3	tortillas, preferably corn, cut into 1-inch (2.5 cm) strips	3
	Vegetable oil	
	Sour cream	
1 to 2	avocados, cut into $\frac{1}{2}$-inch (1 cm) cubes	1 to 2
	Finely chopped red onion	
	Finely chopped cilantro	

1. In a heatproof bowl, soak chili pepper in boiling water for 30 minutes. Drain and discard stem and soaking water. Set aside.

2. In a skillet, cook bacon over medium-high heat until crisp. Drain thoroughly on paper towel. Crumble and set aside, covered, in refrigerator. Drain all but 1 tbsp (15 mL) fat from pan.

3. Reduce heat to medium. Add onions to pan and cook, stirring, until softened. Add garlic, cumin seeds, oregano, lime zest, salt, peppercorns and reserved New Mexico chili and cook, stirring, for 1 minute. Transfer mixture to a food processor along with beans and 1 cup (250 mL) tomato liquid and process until smooth.

4. Transfer to slow cooker stoneware. If you prefer a smooth soup, add remaining tomatoes to food processor and process until smooth; otherwise, chop coarsely before adding to slow cooker stoneware.

5. Add chicken broth. Cover and cook on **Low** for 8 to 10 hours or on **High** for 3 to 4 hours, until mixture is bubbling and flavors are combined. Stir in reserved bacon, mild green chilies and corn. Cover and cook on **High** for 15 to 20 minutes, until corn is heated through.

6. Meanwhile, preheat oven to 400°F (200°C). Brush tortilla strips with oil, place on baking sheet and bake for 4 minutes per side, until crisp and golden.

7. When ready to serve, ladle soup into bowls, lay tortilla strips across surface and top with sour cream, chopped avocado, red onion and cilantro.

PANTRY NOTES

Pinto Beans
Pinto beans are a medium-size, pinky-beige bean often used in Southwestern and Tex-Mex cooking. They have a unique, smoky flavor that marries well with many chilies. Although they lack the pinto bean's earthiness, red kidney or dried Romano beans may be substituted.

Substitutions
Canned beans are a quick and easy substitute for cooked dried beans. For 2 cups (500 mL) cooked beans, use a standard 19-oz (540 mL) can. Drain and rinse well under cold running water before adding to the recipe.

Mixed Mushroom Soup with Creamy Goat Cheese

SERVES 6 TO 8

Here's a rich, tasty soup that is perfect as a starter to an elegant dinner or as the centerpiece of a light meal. The red wine adds depth to the broth, but if you prefer, substitute an equal quantity of broth.

MAKE AHEAD
This dish can be partially prepared the night before it is cooked. Complete Steps 1 through 3. Cover and refrigerate overnight. The next day, continue cooking as directed in Step 4.

1		package ($\frac{1}{2}$ oz/14 g) dried porcini mushrooms	1
1 cup		boiling water	250 mL
2 tbsp		butter, divided	25 mL
1$\frac{1}{2}$ lbs		mixed fresh mushrooms (use a combination of fresh shiitake, cremini and button mushrooms), trimmed and sliced (remove stems from shiitake mushrooms)	750 g
2		onions, finely chopped	2
4		cloves garlic, minced	4
$\frac{1}{2}$ tsp		dried thyme leaves or 2 sprigs fresh thyme	2 mL
1 tsp		salt	5 mL
$\frac{1}{2}$ tsp		cracked black peppercorns	2 mL
1		bay leaf	1
1 cup		dry red wine or vegetable or beef broth	250 mL
4 cups		vegetable or beef broth	1 L
2 tbsp		balsamic vinegar, optional	25 mL
		Whipping cream	
		Crumbled soft goat cheese	
		Finely chopped fresh parsley or chives or fresh thyme leaves	

1. In a heatproof bowl, soak porcini mushrooms in boiling water for 30 minutes. Drain through a fine sieve, reserving liquid. Pat mushrooms dry with paper towel and chop finely. Set aside.

2. In a nonstick skillet, heat 1 tbsp (15 mL) butter over medium heat. Add fresh mushrooms and cook, stirring, until they lose their liquid. Transfer to slow cooker stoneware.

3. In same pan, melt remaining butter. Add onions and cook, stirring, until softened. Add reserved porcini mushrooms, garlic, thyme, salt and peppercorns and cook, stirring, for 1 minute. Transfer to slow cooker stoneware. Add bay leaf, wine, broth and reserved mushroom soaking liquid and stir to combine.

4. Cover and cook on **Low** for 6 to 8 hours or on **High** for 3 to 4 hours. Discard bay leaf. Stir in balsamic vinegar, if using.

5. When ready to serve, ladle soup into individual bowls. Drizzle with cream, sprinkle with goat cheese and garnish with fresh herbs, as desired.

Mulligatawny Soup

SERVES 8

Mulligatawny, which means "pepper water" in Tamil, is an Anglo-Indian soup, imported to England by seafaring merchants. It is usually made with chicken, but a vegetarian version was documented by the great English cook Eliza Acton in her book Modern Cookery, *published in 1845. This adaptation can be varied to include chicken. Using potatoes rather than rice is a departure from the norm as is the option of adding cauliflower along with, or instead of, chicken. This is a hearty and tasty soup that is suitable for many occasions, either as a first course or the focal point of a light meal.*

1 tbsp	vegetable oil	15 mL
2	onions, finely chopped	2
2	carrots, peeled and thinly sliced	2
4	stalks celery, peeled and thinly sliced	4
4	cloves garlic, minced	4
1 tbsp	curry powder	15 mL
1 tsp	cumin seeds	5 mL
1 tsp	salt	5 mL
½ tsp	cracked black peppercorns	2 mL
2	medium potatoes, peeled and diced	2
5 cups	vegetable broth	1.25 L
1 cup	whipping cream or plain yogurt	250 mL
2 cups	cooked cauliflower florets, optional	500 mL
	Finely chopped cilantro or parsley	

1. In a skillet, heat oil over medium heat. Add onions, carrots and celery and cook, stirring, until softened. Add garlic, curry powder, cumin seeds, salt and peppercorns and cook, stirring, for 1 minute. Add potatoes and broth and bring to a boil. Transfer to slow cooker stoneware.

2. Cover and cook on **Low** for 8 to 10 hours or on **High** for 4 to 5 hours, until vegetables are tender. In a blender or food processor, purée soup in batches and return to slow cooker stoneware. Or, using a hand-held blender, purée the soup in stoneware. Stir in cream and cauliflower, if using. Cover and cook on **High** for 30 minutes, until heated through.

3. When ready to serve, ladle into bowls and garnish with cilantro.

VARIATION

Chicken Mulligatawny Soup: This is a great way to use up leftover chicken. Use chicken broth instead of vegetable broth and stir in 8 oz (250 g) cooked chicken (shredded or diced) along with, or instead of, the cauliflower.

MAKE AHEAD
This soup can be partially prepared the night before it is cooked. Complete Step 1. Do not add potatoes. Cover and refrigerate mixture overnight. The next morning, stir in potatoes and continue cooking as directed in Step 2.

Versatile Garlic Soup

SERVES 6
·······························

Garlic soup, which is Spanish in origin, provides a tasty base that lends itself to many variations. I like to drizzle the freshly made soup with pesto. If I have leftovers, I add cream or a broiled cheese topping to mitigate the flavor of the garlic, which intensifies when the soup is refrigerated.

2 tbsp	butter	25 mL
15	large cloves garlic, peeled	15
2	leeks, white part only, cleaned and thinly sliced (see Tip, page 203)	2
½ tsp	dried thyme leaves	2 mL
½ tsp	freshly grated nutmeg	2 mL
1 tsp	salt	5 mL
½ tsp	cracked black peppercorns	2 mL
3	potatoes, peeled and diced	3
6 cups	vegetable or chicken broth	1.5 L
	Pesto, optional	

1. In a skillet, melt butter oil over medium-low heat. Add garlic and cook, stirring frequently, until golden and softened. Using a slotted spoon, transfer to slow cooker stoneware. Add leeks to pan and cook, stirring, until softened. Add thyme, nutmeg, salt and peppercorns and cook, stirring, for 1 minute. Transfer to slow cooker stoneware. Add potatoes and broth and stir to combine.

2. Cover and cook on **Low** for 8 to 10 hours or on **High** for 4 to 5 hours. Strain vegetables, reserving broth. In a blender or food processor, purée vegetables with 1 cup (250 mL) reserved broth until smooth. Return mixture, along with reserved broth, to slow cooker stoneware and stir well.

3. When ready to serve, ladle into warm bowls and drizzle with pesto, if using.

···

VARIATIONS
Creamy Garlic Soup: Add 1 cup (250 mL) whipping cream to puréed soup.
Cheesy Garlic Soup: Preheat broiler. Ladle soup into ovenproof bowls. Place 2 slices of baguette in each bowl. Sprinkle liberally with shredded Swiss or Gruyère cheese and broil for 2 to 3 minutes, until top is bubbly and brown. Serve immediately.

Kale with Smoked Sausage Soup

SERVES 6 TO 8

....

Here's a hearty, nutritious and delicious soup that works as the centerpiece of a soup-and-salad dinner. On busy evenings, you can leave it in the slow cooker on Warm and family members can help themselves. I like to serve this with dark rye bread and a salad of grated carrots with a lemon juice and olive oil vinaigrette. If you're feeling festive, toss some orange slices with the carrots.

MAKE AHEAD
This soup can be partially prepared the night before it is cooked. Complete Steps 1 and 2. Cover and refrigerate overnight. The next morning, continue cooking as directed in Step 3.

2	slices bacon	2
2	onions, finely chopped	2
2	cloves garlic, minced	2
1	fresh chili pepper, finely chopped (see Tips, page 54), optional	1
1 tsp	dried oregano leaves	5 mL
1 tsp	salt	5 mL
½ tsp	cracked black peppercorns	2 mL
2 tbsp	white vinegar	25 mL
8 cups	chicken broth	2 L
1	can (19 oz/540 mL) white beans or black-eyed peas or 1 cup (250 mL) dried white beans or black-eyed peas, cooked and drained (see Basic Beans, page 214)	1
1 lb	kale, trimmed of stems and center ribs and coarsely chopped	500 g
1 lb	cooked smoked sausage, such as kielbasa or cured chorizo, sliced and chopped into bite-size pieces	500 g

1. In a skillet, cook bacon over medium-high heat until crisp. Drain thoroughly on paper towel. Crumble and refrigerate, covered, until ready to use. Drain all but 1 tbsp (15 mL) fat from pan.

2. Add onions to pan and cook, stirring, until softened. Add garlic, chili pepper, if using, oregano, salt and peppercorns and cook, stirring, for 1 minute. Stir in vinegar and transfer mixture to slow cooker stoneware.

3. Add broth, beans and kale and stir to combine. Cover and cook on **Low** for 8 hours or on **High** for 4 hours, until kale is softened and mixture is bubbling. (If you prefer a smooth soup, purée mixture before adding the sausage.) Stir in sausage and reserved bacon, if using. Cover and cook on **High** for 30 minutes, until sausage is heated through.

continued on page 54

TIPS

• Don't be alarmed when you place the kale in the slow cooker. It reduces dramatically in volume when cooked.

• Almost any variety of fresh hot pepper works well in this soup. I prefer the long red chili used in Indian cuisine, but I've also had good success with half a habanero chili. (Don't use a whole one unless you're wild about heat.)

• If you happen to have a boot of Parmesan in your refrigerator (the piece of tough rind that is left over from Parmesan cheese), add it to the soup along with the broth, for additional flavor and a creamy note.

VARIATIONS

Greens with Smoked Sausage Soup: Substitute an equal quantity of collard greens for the kale.

Kale with Smoked Sausage Soup and Crusty Cheese: Ladle hot soup into heatproof bowls. Top with sliced baguette and a thick layer of shredded Swiss cheese. Place under preheated broiler until cheese is melted and brown.

Kale with Turkey Kielbasa: For a lower-fat version of this soup, omit the bacon and soften the vegetables in 1 tbsp (15 mL) vegetable oil. Use turkey kielbasa rather than kielbasa made from pork.

Ribollita

SERVES 6 AS A MAIN COURSE OR 8 AS A STARTER

Originally intended as a method for using up leftover minestrone — hence the name ribollita, which means "twice cooked" — this hearty Italian soup has acquired an illustrious reputation of its own. The distinguishing ingredient is country-style bread, which is added to the soup and cooked in the broth. Drizzled with olive oil and sprinkled with grated Parmesan cheese, this makes a satisfying light meal or tasty starter to an Italian-themed dinner.

MAKE AHEAD
Cook this soup overnight or the day before you intend to serve it. Refrigerate until you are ready to serve, then reheat in the oven (see Tips, below).

1	can (19 oz/540 mL) white kidney beans, drained and rinsed, or 1 cup (250 mL) dried white kidney beans, cooked and drained (see Basic Beans, page 214)	1
5 cups	vegetable or chicken broth, divided	1.25 L
1 tbsp	vegetable oil	15 mL
2	onions, finely chopped	2
2	carrots, peeled and diced	2
2	stalks celery, peeled and diced	2
4	cloves garlic, minced	4
1/4 cup	finely chopped parsley	50 mL
1	long red chili pepper, minced, optional	1
1 tbsp	grated lemon zest	15 mL
1 tsp	finely chopped fresh rosemary leaves or dried rosemary leaves, crumbled	5 mL
1 tsp	salt	5 mL
1/2 tsp	cracked black peppercorns	2 mL
2	potatoes, peeled and grated	2
1	bunch Swiss chard, stems and veins removed and coarsely chopped	1
3	thick slices day-old country-style bread	3
	Extra-virgin olive oil	
	Freshly grated Parmesan cheese	

1. In a food processor, combine beans with 1 cup (250 mL) broth and purée until smooth. Set aside.

2. In a skillet, heat oil over medium heat. Add onions, carrots and celery and cook, stirring, until softened. Add garlic, parsley, chili pepper, if using, lemon zest, rosemary, salt and peppercorns and cook, stirring, for 1 minute. Add bean mixture and bring to a boil.

3. Transfer mixture to slow cooker stoneware. Stir in potatoes and remaining broth. Cover and cook on **Low** for 8 to 10 hours or on **High** for 4 to 5 hours. Stir in Swiss chard and bread. Cover and cook on **High** for 30 minutes, until chard is cooked.

4. When ready to serve, ladle into bowls, breaking bread into pieces. Drizzle with extra-virgin olive oil and sprinkle with Parmesan.

TIPS
• Although I prefer the bit of heat that the chili pepper adds, the soup will be flavorful without it.
• Traditionally, ribollita is reheated in the oven. Ladle the soup into ovenproof bowls, drizzle with olive oil and sprinkle with Parmesan. Bake in a preheated oven (350°F/180°C) for about 30 minutes, until the top is lightly browned.

Mexican Chicken Soup

SERVES 6

Here's a surprisingly simple, yet absolutely delicious, soup that is light and refreshing. Topped with avocado and a cumin-flavored cream, it is distinctive enough to impress discriminating guests.

MAKE AHEAD
Chop the vegetables and hot pepper. Cover and refrigerate until you are ready to cook.

Broth

2	onions, chopped	2
4	stalks celery, peeled and chopped	4
2	carrots, peeled and chopped	2
2	sprigs cilantro	2
1	hot chili pepper, seeded and chopped (see Tips, below)	1
10	whole peppercorns	10
1 tsp	salt	5 mL
2	half chicken breasts, each cut in half	2
1	can (10 oz/284 mL) condensed chicken broth	1
5 cups	water	1.25 L

Topping

½ cup	whipping cream	125 mL
1 tbsp	cumin seeds, toasted and ground (see Tips, below)	15 mL
2	small avocados, sliced	2
	Lime juice	
	Finely chopped cilantro	

1. In slow cooker stoneware, combine ingredients for broth. Cover and cook on **Low** for 6 hours or on **High** for 3 hours, until chicken is falling off the bone. Lift out chicken and remove skin and bones. Shred by pulling the meat apart with two forks and keep warm. Strain broth through a fine sieve, discard solids and keep warm.

2. Topping: In a bowl, whip cream. Beat in cumin seeds and set aside.

3. Ladle broth into six warm bowls. Lay shredded chicken and avocado strips on top. Sprinkle with lime juice. Top with a dollop of cream and garnish with cilantro. Serve immediately.

TIPS
• To toast cumin seeds: Place in a dry skillet over medium heat and cook, stirring, until lightly browned and aroma is released. Immediately transfer to a small bowl. When cool, grind seeds in a spice grinder, with a rolling pin or in a mortar with a pestle.
• Jalapeño, habanero and long red chili peppers all work well in this recipe, although they deliver varying degrees of heat and different flavors.

Beef and Barley Soup with Mushrooms

SERVES 6

....

This hearty, stick-to-the-ribs soup is a perfect pick-me-up after a day in the chilly outdoors. If you have really worked up an appetite, add the Swiss cheese topping. Serve with crusty rolls and a tossed salad for a great winter meal.

MAKE AHEAD
This soup can be partially assembled the night before it is cooked. Complete Steps 1 and 3, heating oil before adding vegetables to pan. Cover and refrigerate overnight. The next morning, brown beef, or if you're pressed for time, omit this step and add to mixture. Continue with Step 4. Alternately, the dish may be cooked overnight and refrigerated until you are ready to serve. Reheat in a saucepan on the stovetop.

1	package (1/2 oz/14 g) dried wild mushrooms, such as porcini	1
1 cup	boiling water	250 mL
1 tbsp	vegetable oil	15 mL
8 oz	stewing beef, cut into 1/4-inch (0.5 cm) dice	250 g
2	onions, finely chopped	2
2	stalks celery, peeled and thinly sliced	2
2	carrots, peeled and diced	2
2	cloves garlic, minced	2
1 tsp	salt	5 mL
1/2 tsp	cracked black peppercorns	2 mL
1/2 tsp	dried thyme leaves	2 mL
1	bay leaf	1
1/2 cup	pearl barley, rinsed	125 mL
2 tbsp	tomato paste	25 mL
6 cups	beef broth	1.5 L
	Sour cream	
	Finely chopped dill	

1. In a heatproof bowl, soak dried mushrooms in boiling water for 30 minutes, then strain through a fine sieve, reserving liquid. Chop mushrooms finely and set aside.

2. In a skillet, heat oil over medium-high heat. Add beef and cook, stirring, until lightly browned. Using a slotted spoon, transfer to slow cooker stoneware.

3. Add onions, celery and carrots to pan and cook, stirring, until softened. Add garlic, salt, peppercorns, thyme and bay leaf and cook, stirring, for 1 minute. Add barley and stir until coated. Stir in tomato paste, beef broth and reserved mushroom liquid and bring to a boil. Transfer to slow cooker stoneware.

4. Cover and cook on **Low** for 6 to 8 hours or on **High** for 3 to 4 hours. Discard bay leaf. Ladle into individual bowls, top with a dollop of sour cream and garnish with dill.

....

VARIATION
Beef and Barley Soup with Cheese: Instead of finishing the soup with sour cream and dill, ladle into ovenproof bowls. Place a slice or two of baguette in each bowl. Sprinkle liberally with shredded Swiss cheese and broil for 2 to 3 minutes, until top is bubbly and brown.

International Split Pea Soup

SERVES 6 TO 8

There are many variations on the basic theme of split pea soup. Made with split green peas and a ham bone or ham hock, it is an American classic, apparently imported to the colonies by early Dutch settlers. In Canada, it is a traditional Quebec dish, made with split yellow peas and flavored with salt pork. Citizens of the Middle East are likely to enjoy a vegetarian version, seasoned with cumin and lemon. This recipe borrows a bit from each of these cuisines. I like to serve this soup steaming hot with plenty of fresh, dark bread, coleslaw and sliced Cheddar cheese. It makes a great winter meal.

MAKE AHEAD
This soup can be cooked overnight, then refrigerated until ready to serve.

2 cups	split yellow peas, soaked, drained and rinsed (see Tips, below)	500 mL
2	onions, diced	2
4	stalks celery, peeled and thinly sliced	4
3	carrots, peeled and diced	3
2	potatoes, peeled and diced	2
1	smoked ham hock	1
6 cups	water	1.5 L
1 tbsp	cumin seeds	15 mL
1 tsp	salt	5 mL
½ tsp	cracked black peppercorns	2 mL
¼ cup	freshly squeezed lemon juice	50 mL
¼ cup	finely chopped parsley	50 mL

1. In slow cooker stoneware, combine all ingredients except lemon juice and parsley. Cover and cook on **Low** for 8 to 10 hours or on **High** for 4 to 5 hours, until peas are tender. Remove ham hock and stir in lemon juice. Ladle into bowls and garnish with parsley.

TIPS

• I've found that yellow split peas need to be well soaked before being cooked in the slow cooker. Bring the peas and 6 cups (1.5 L) water to a boil. Boil rapidly for 3 minutes, then turn the heat off and let sit for 1 hour. Drain and rinse before adding to the recipe.

• Smoked ham hocks are available from butchers and can often be found in the meat section of well-stocked supermarkets. They are wonderful flavor enhancers, particularly for legumes.

VARIATION

Southwestern-Style Split Pea Soup: In a heatproof bowl, soak 2 New Mexico chilies in 2 cups (500 mL) boiling water for 30 minutes. Drain and discard liquid and stems. Chop finely. After the soup has cooked for 6 hours on Low or 4 hours on High, add the chopped reconstituted chilies to the slow cooker. If desired, add 1 finely chopped jalapeño pepper at the same time. To serve, top with sour cream and garnish with finely chopped cilantro instead of parsley.

Beef and Veal

Best-Ever Meatballs in Tomato Sauce

Best-Ever Meatballs in Tomato Sauce

SERVES 8

....

I love the flavor of these savory meatballs, which are seasoned with cumin and oregano. A hint of cinnamon in the simple tomato sauce adds an intriguing note. Although they are delicious over spaghetti, the traditional combination, I also like to serve these tasty nuggets over steaming hot couscous or baked potatoes, cut into quarters.

MAKE AHEAD
This dish can be partially prepared the night before it is cooked. Complete Step 3, adding 1 tbsp (15 mL) oil to pan before softening onions. Cover and refrigerate. The next day, make the meatballs and continue cooking as directed in Steps 1, 2 and 4.

Meatballs

¼ cup	long-grain converted rice	50 mL
2 lbs	lean ground beef	1 kg
2	eggs, beaten	2
1	onion, grated	1
2	cloves garlic, minced	2
1 tsp	dried oregano leaves	5 mL
1 tsp	ground cumin	5 mL
½ tsp	salt	2 mL
¼ tsp	freshly ground black pepper	1 mL
2 tbsp	vegetable oil	25 mL

Tomato Sauce

2	onions, finely chopped	2
4	cloves garlic, minced	4
2 tsp	dried oregano leaves	10 mL
1 tsp	salt	5 mL
½ tsp	cracked black peppercorns	2 mL
1	cinnamon stick piece, about 2 inches (5 cm)	1
1	can (28 oz/796 mL) tomatoes	1
2 tbsp	lemon juice	25 mL

1. Meatballs: In a bowl, stir rice into 4 cups (1 L) boiling water. Set aside for 30 minutes to soak. Drain well. Return rice to bowl. Add remaining ingredients, except for oil, and mix well. Form into 16 balls, each approximately 2 inches (5 cm) in diameter.

2. In a skillet, heat oil over medium-high heat. Add meatballs, in batches, and brown on all sides. Transfer to slow cooker stoneware. Drain all but 1 tbsp (15 mL) fat from pan. (If you used extra-lean ground beef, you may have to add oil.)

3. Tomato Sauce: Reduce heat to medium. Add onions to pan and cook, stirring, until softened. Add garlic, oregano, salt, peppercorns and cinnamon stick and cook, stirring, for 1 minute. Stir in tomatoes and lemon juice and bring to a boil, breaking up tomatoes with a spoon as they cook.

4. Pour sauce over meatballs. Cover and cook on **Low** for 8 hours or on **High** for 4 hours, until meatballs are no longer pink inside. Discard cinnamon stick.

Beef and Rigatoni Bake

SERVES 6 TO 8

....

This is a nice weekday meal. It is particularly suitable for those evenings when everyone is coming and going at different times. You can leave the fixings for salad out, set the slow cooker to Warm and let people help themselves.

MAKE AHEAD
This dish can be partially prepared the night before it is cooked. Complete Steps 1 and 2, refrigerating meat and vegetable mixtures separately. The next morning, combine in slow cooker stoneware and continue cooking as directed.

2 tbsp	vegetable oil, divided	25 mL
2 lbs	lean ground beef	1 kg
2	onions, finely chopped	2
4	stalks celery, peeled and thinly sliced	4
4	cloves garlic, minced	4
1	fresh hot chili pepper, minced, optional	1
1/2 tsp	dried thyme leaves	2 mL
1/2 tsp	salt	2 mL
1/2 tsp	cracked black peppercorns	2 mL
1	can (10 oz/284 mL) condensed tomato soup	1
1 cup	tomato juice, beef stock or water	250 mL
2 tbsp	Worcestershire sauce	25 mL
4 cups	rigatoni, cooked until barely tender (about 7 minutes) and drained	1 L
2 cups	shredded Cheddar cheese	500 mL
1	green bell pepper, seeded and finely chopped, optional	1

1. In a skillet, heat 1 tbsp (15 mL) oil over medium-high heat. Add beef and cook, breaking up with a wooden spoon, until no longer pink. Using a slotted spoon, transfer to slow cooker stoneware. Drain liquid from pan.

2. Reduce heat to medium. Add remaining oil to pan. Add onions and celery and cook, stirring, until softened. Add garlic, chili pepper, if using, thyme, salt and peppercorns and cook, stirring, for 1 minute. Stir in tomato soup, juice and Worcestershire sauce. Transfer to slow cooker stoneware. Add cooked rigatoni and stir well.

3. Cover and cook on **Low** for 8 hours or on **High** for 4 hours, until hot and bubbly. Stir in cheese and green pepper, if using. Cover and cook on **High** for 20 minutes, until cheese is melted and pepper is heated through.

Italian-Style Pot Roast with Polenta

SERVES 6 TO 8

Although pot roast is not a dish I automatically associate with Italian cuisine, there are many regional Italian recipes that involve braising less tender cuts of beef in copious quantities of a local red wine. This delicious slow cooker pot roast falls into that tradition. Serve the mouth-watering sauce over hot polenta.

1 tbsp	vegetable oil	15 mL
1	beef pot roast, about 3 to 4 lbs (1.5 to 2 kg), patted dry	1
2 oz	pancetta or sliced bacon (see Tip, below)	60 g
2	onions, finely chopped	2
2	carrots, peeled and thinly sliced	2
2	stalks celery, peeled and thinly sliced	2
2	cloves garlic, minced	2
1 tsp	salt	5 mL
½ tsp	cracked black peppercorns	2 mL
4	whole cloves	4
2	bay leaves	2
1	cinnamon stick piece, about 2 inches (5 cm)	1
2 tbsp	tomato paste	25 mL
1 cup	dry red wine	250 mL
½ cup	small black olives, pitted	125 mL
	Slow-Cooked Polenta (see recipe, page 211)	

MAKE AHEAD
This dish can be partially prepared the night before it is cooked. Complete Step 2, heating 1 tbsp (15 mL) oil in pan before softening onions. Cover and refrigerate overnight. The next morning, brown roast (Step 1), or if you're pressed for time, omit this step and place meat directly in slow cooker stoneware. Continue cooking as directed in Step 3.

1. In a nonstick skillet, heat oil over medium-high heat. Add roast and brown in skillet on all sides. Transfer to slow cooker stoneware.

2. Reduce heat to medium. Add pancetta, onions, carrots and celery to pan and cook, stirring, until softened. Add garlic, salt, peppercorns, cinnamon stick, cloves and bay leaves and cook, stirring, for 1 minute. Stir in tomato paste and wine and bring to a boil.

3. Pour mixture over roast, making sure that it thoroughly coats the meat. Cover and cook on **Low** for 10 to 12 hours or on **High** for 5 to 6 hours, until meat is very tender. Remove roast from slow cooker and keep warm. Pour cooking liquid into a saucepan and simmer on medium heat until reduced by one-third. Taste and adjust seasoning. Add olives and heat through. Discard bay leaves and cinnamon stick.

4. Meanwhile, spread polenta over bottom of a deep platter. Slice roast and layer slices over top of polenta. Pour sauce over meat and serve any extra in a separate sauceboat. Serve piping hot.

TIP
• If you are using bacon in this recipe, I recommend that you spoon off most of the fat before adding the tomato paste and wine.

Home-Style Pot Roast

SERVES 6 TO 8

I love this recipe — it is so delicious and easy to make. The secret ingredient is a flavorful steak sauce. I prefer HP Sauce, a British brand, but any well-loved variety will do. Be sure to include mounds of steamy mashed potatoes to soak up the mouth-watering sauce.

MAKE AHEAD
This dish can be partially prepared the night before it is cooked. Complete Step 2, heating 1 tbsp (15 mL) oil in pan before softening vegetables. Cover and refrigerate overnight. The next morning, brown the roast (Step 1), or if you're pressed for time, skip this step and place meat directly in slow cooker stoneware. Continue cooking as directed in Step 3.

1 tbsp	vegetable oil	15 mL
1	beef pot roast, about 3 to 4 lbs (1.5 to 2 kg)	1
2	onions, thinly sliced	2
4	stalks celery, peeled and thinly sliced	4
2	cloves garlic, minced	2
1/2 tsp	dried thyme leaves	2 mL
1 tsp	salt	5 mL
1/2 tsp	cracked black peppercorns	2 mL
1/4 cup	all-purpose flour	50 mL
1	can (10 oz/284 mL) condensed beef broth, undiluted	1
1	bay leaf	1
1 to 2	green bell peppers, seeded and finely chopped	1 to 2
3 tbsp	steak sauce	45 mL

1. In a nonstick skillet, heat oil over medium-high heat. Pat roast dry with paper towel and brown in skillet on all sides. Transfer to slow cooker stoneware.

2. Reduce heat to medium. Add onions and celery and cook, stirring, until softened. Add garlic, thyme, salt and peppercorns and cook, stirring, for 1 minute. Add flour and cook, stirring, for 1 minute. Add beef broth and bay leaf and cook, stirring, until mixture thickens.

3. Pour mixture over roast. Cover and cook on **Low** for 10 to 12 hours or on **High** for 5 to 6 hours, until meat is tender. Stir green peppers and steak sauce into gravy. Cover and cook on **High** for 30 minutes, until peppers are soft. To serve, discard bay leaf, place roast on a deep platter and spoon sauce over top.

TIP
• If you feel the gravy is not thick enough after the roast has finished cooking, add a flour thickener. Transfer the meat to a deep platter and keep warm. Pour the sauce into a saucepan and heat slowly. Meanwhile, in a small mixing bowl, place 2 tbsp (25 mL) all-purpose flour. Add the sauce, a tablespoonful (15 mL) at a time, stirring after each addition, until mixture is smooth. When you have about 1/2 cup (125 mL), add the mixture to the saucepan and bring to a boil over medium-low heat, stirring constantly, until the sauce thickens. Pour over roast and serve.

Sauerbraten

SERVES 6 TO 8

....

*Sauerbraten is a
German-style pot roast,
which is usually
marinated for several
days in the refrigerator
before it is cooked. I've
found that using the
slow cooker enables me
to eliminate this
tiresome step and still
achieve excellent results.
However, for optimum
flavor, the roast should
be turned halfway
through the cooking
time to give all parts of
the meat equal exposure
to the cooking broth.*

MAKE AHEAD
This dish can be
partially prepared
the night before it
is cooked. Complete
Step 2, heating 1 tbsp
(15 mL) oil in pan
before softening
vegetables. Cover and
refrigerate overnight.
The next morning,
brown roast (Step 1),
or if you're pressed
for time, omit this
step and place roast
directly in slow cooker
stoneware. Continue
cooking as directed
in Step 3.

1 tbsp	vegetable oil	1
1	beef pot roast, about 4 to 5 lbs (2 to 2.5 kg)	1
2	onions, thinly sliced	2
4	stalks celery, peeled and thinly sliced	4
4	carrots, peeled and cut into ½-inch (1 cm) cubes	4
2	cloves garlic, minced	2
1 tsp	salt	5 mL
1 tsp	cracked black peppercorns	5 mL
6	whole cloves	6
2 tbsp	all-purpose flour	25 mL
1 cup	cider vinegar	250 mL
1½ cups	beef stock	375 mL
1	bay leaf	1
¼ cup	packed brown sugar	50 mL
12	gingersnap cookies, crumbled	12
½ cup	sour cream	125 mL

1. In a nonstick skillet, heat oil over medium-high heat. Pat roast dry with paper towel and brown in skillet on all sides. Transfer to slow cooker stoneware.

2. Reduce heat to medium. Add onions, celery and carrots to pan and cook, stirring, until vegetables are softened. Add garlic, salt, peppercorns and cloves and cook, stirring, for 1 minute. Sprinkle mixture with flour and stir. Add vinegar, beef stock and bay leaf and bring to a boil.

3. Pour mixture over roast. Cover and cook on **Low** for 10 to 12 hours or on **High** for 5 to 6 hours, until meat is very tender. Remove roast from slow cooker and place on serving platter. Discard bay leaf. Add brown sugar and stir until dissolved. Stir in gingersnaps and sour cream. Pour some sauce over roast and pass the remainder in a sauceboat. Serve piping hot.

Classic Beef Stew

SERVES 6

······························

When I was growing up, one of my favorite dishes was my mother's beef stew. There was nothing fancy about it — just basic meat and vegetable combinations — but the house always smelled so good while it was cooking, and it was deliciously comforting on a cold winter's day. This is the stew I've tried to capture in this recipe. That said, I must confess that even Mom's stew can be improved upon with the addition of mushrooms cooked in Madeira.

1 tbsp	vegetable oil	15 mL
2 lbs	stewing beef, cut into 1-inch (2.5 cm) cubes and patted dry	1 kg
2	large onions, finely chopped	2
4	stalks celery, peeled and diced	4
2	large carrots, peeled and diced	2
2	cloves garlic, minced	2
1 tsp	dried thyme leaves	5 mL
1 tsp	salt	5 mL
½ tsp	cracked black peppercorns	2 mL
¼ cup	all-purpose flour	50 mL
1	can (10 oz/284 mL) condensed beef broth, undiluted	1
½ cup	dry red wine or water	125 mL
2	bay leaves	2
	Finely chopped fresh parsley	

1. In a nonstick skillet, heat oil over medium-high heat. Add beef, in batches, and brown on all sides. Using a slotted spoon, transfer to slow cooker stoneware.

2. Reduce heat to medium. Add onions, celery and carrots and cook, stirring, until vegetables are softened. Add garlic, thyme, salt and peppercorns and cook, stirring, for 1 minute. Add flour and cook, stirring, for 1 minute. Add beef broth and wine and cook, stirring, until thickened. Add bay leaves.

3. Transfer mixture to slow cooker stoneware and stir thoroughly to combine ingredients. Cover and cook on **Low** for 8 to 10 hours or on **High** for 4 to 5 hours, until beef is very tender. Discard bay leaves. Just before serving, garnish liberally with parsley.

···

VARIATIONS

Classic Beef Stew with Madeira Mushrooms: In a nonstick skillet, melt 2 tbsp (25 mL) butter over medium heat. Add 12 oz (375 g) sliced button mushrooms and cook until mushrooms release their liquid. Season to taste, then sprinkle with 1 tbsp (15 mL) all-purpose flour. Cook, stirring, for 1 minute. Add ¼ cup (50 mL) Madeira or port wine and stir until thickened. Just before serving, stir into stew, then garnish with parsley.

Beef Stew with Roasted Garlic: Mash 6 cloves roasted garlic (see Tips, page 22) and stir into stew before garnishing with parsley.

Brisket of Beef in Tomato Onion Gravy

SERVES 8 TO 10

Brisket is one of those old-fashioned cuts of meat that never lose their appeal. It is the basis for several versions of good old American barbecue, traditional cholent, eaten on the Sabbath by Orthodox Jews, and seasoned Irish corned beef. This brisket couldn't be any easier to make. Serve with hot mashed potatoes to soak up the sauce and a green vegetable such as broccoli or green beans.

¼ cup	all-purpose flour	50 mL
1	double beef brisket (4 to 5 lbs/2 to 2.5 kg), trimmed	1
1	package (1½ oz/40 g) dry onion soup mix	1
½ tsp	cracked black peppercorns	2 mL
1	can (10 oz/284 mL) condensed tomato soup	1
¼ cup	beef stock or water	50 mL
2 tbsp	packed brown sugar	25 mL
2 tbsp	balsamic or red wine vinegar	25 mL
	Additional all-purpose flour (see Tip, below), optional	

1. Rub flour into brisket on both sides and place in slow cooker stoneware.

2. In a bowl, combine onion soup mix, peppercorns, tomato soup and beef stock. Pour mixture over brisket. Cover and cook on **Low** for 12 hours or on **High** for 6 hours, until beef is very tender. Transfer brisket to a deep platter and slice thinly. Stir brown sugar and vinegar into sauce. Pour over sliced meat or pass separately in a sauceboat.

TIP
• If you prefer a thicker gravy, keep the cooked brisket warm and pour the sauce into a saucepan. Place 2 tbsp (25 mL) all-purpose flour in a small bowl. Add ¼ cup (50 mL) hot cooking liquid, 2 tbsp (25 mL) at a time, stirring to thoroughly blend after each addition. Stir mixture into remaining sauce and cook, stirring, over medium heat until thickened. Pour over brisket and serve.

MAKE AHEAD
You can cook the brisket overnight. Once cooked, refrigerate immediately. When meat is cool, slice thinly. Place in a Dutch oven, cover with sauce and reheat on stovetop over medium-low heat until hot and bubbling. Serve immediately.

Brisket of Beef with Horseradish Gravy

SERVES 8 TO 10

....

This succulent brisket owes its inspiration to English cooking, where roast beef is traditionally served with horseradish. Serve with mounds of hot mashed potatoes to soak up the sauce.

MAKE AHEAD
This dish can be partially prepared the night before it is cooked. Complete Step 2, heating 1 tbsp (15 mL) oil in pan before softening onions. Cover and refrigerate overnight. The next morning, brown brisket, or if you're pressed for time, omit this step and add meat directly to slow cooker stoneware. Continue cooking as directed in Step 3. Or you can cook the brisket overnight. Once cooked, refrigerate immediately. When meat is cool, slice thinly. Place in a Dutch oven, cover with sauce and reheat on stovetop over medium-low heat until hot and bubbling. Serve immediately.

1 tbsp	vegetable oil	15 mL
1	double beef brisket (4 to 5 lbs/2 to 2.5 kg), trimmed	1
2	onions, finely chopped	2
4	cloves garlic, minced	4
1 tbsp	paprika	15 mL
1 tsp	dried thyme leaves	5 mL
1 tsp	salt	5 mL
1 tsp	cracked black peppercorns	5 mL
1/4 cup	all-purpose flour	50 mL
1 1/2 cups	beef stock	375 mL
2 tbsp	freshly grated horseradish or 1 1/2 tbsp (22 mL) prepared horseradish, drained	25 mL
1 tbsp	Dijon mustard	15 mL
1/4 cup	finely chopped green onion	50 mL
1/2 cup	whipping cream	125 mL

1. In a nonstick skillet, heat oil over medium-high heat. Add brisket and brown on both sides. Transfer to slow cooker stoneware.

2. Reduce heat to medium. Add onions and cook until softened. Add garlic, paprika, thyme, salt and peppercorns and cook, stirring, for 1 minute. Sprinkle flour over mixture and cook, stirring, for 1 minute. Add beef stock and cook, stirring, until thickened.

3. Pour mixture over brisket. Cover and cook on **Low** for 12 hours, until meat is very tender. Transfer brisket to a deep platter. Stir horseradish, mustard, green onion and cream into gravy and pour over meat. To serve, slice meat thinly across the grain and top with gravy.

....

TIP
• If you prefer a thicker gravy, see Tip, page 70.

Tamale Pie with Chili Cornmeal Crust

SERVES 8

·······························

Here is a hearty dish that is terrific for a buffet table. All it needs is a tossed salad and ice cold beer.

MAKE AHEAD
This dish can be partially prepared the night before it is cooked. Complete Steps 1 and 2. Cover and refrigerate cooked meat separately from vegetable mixture. The next morning, continue cooking as directed in Step 3.

Base

1 tbsp	vegetable oil	15 mL
1 lb	lean ground beef	500 g
1 lb	Italian sausage, removed from casings	500 g
2	onions, finely chopped	2
2	carrots, peeled and diced	2
2	stalks celery, peeled and diced	2
1	jalapeño pepper, optional	1
1 tbsp	chili powder	15 mL
1 tbsp	cumin seeds	15 mL
1 tbsp	dried oregano leaves	15 mL
1 tsp	salt	5 mL
½ tsp	cracked black peppercorns	2 mL
1 cup	ketchup	250 mL
1	can (14 oz/398 mL) refried beans	1
1 cup	beef stock	250 mL
1½ cups	corn kernels	375 mL

Topping

1 cup	cornmeal	250 mL
½ cup	all-purpose flour	125 mL
2 tsp	baking powder	10 mL
½ tsp	salt	2 mL
¼ tsp	freshly ground black pepper	1 mL
1 cup	milk	250 mL
¼ cup	melted butter	50 mL
1	egg, beaten	1
1 cup	shredded Monterey Jack cheese	250 mL
1	can (4.5 oz/127 mL) chopped mild green chilies, including juice	1

1. In a skillet, heat oil over medium-high heat. Cook beef and sausage, in batches, breaking up with a wooden spoon, until no longer pink. Using a slotted spoon, transfer to slow cooker stoneware. Drain all but 1 tbsp (15 mL) liquid from pan.

continued on page 74

2. Reduce heat to medium. Add onions, carrots and celery to pan and cook, stirring, until softened. Add jalapeño pepper, if using, chili powder, cumin seeds, oregano, salt and peppercorns and cook, stirring, for 1 minute. Stir in ketchup and refried beans, breaking up beans with a spoon until they are well integrated into mixture. Add stock and corn and bring to a boil.

3. Transfer to slow cooker stoneware and stir well.

4. Topping: In a bowl, mix together dry ingredients. Make a well in the center. Add milk, butter and egg and mix until just blended with dry ingredients. Stir in cheese and chilies. Spread mixture evenly over filling. Cover and cook on **Low** for 6 to 8 hours or on **High** for 3 to 4 hours, until top is risen and crusty and meat mixture is bubbling and hot.

TIP
• Use sweet or hot Italian sausage in this recipe depending on your preference.

PANTRY NOTES

Chili Peppers
Chili peppers are an invaluable asset in any kitchen. In addition to piquancy, chilies add complexity to sauces, and their judicious use can easily transform a recipe from run-of-the-mill to delicious. Now widely available in supermarkets and specialty stores, chilies come in a diverse range of temperatures and flavors. Some are only mildly hot, others are incendiary, and their tastes range from smoky and nutty to fruity.

Creamy Beef Curry

This is a very simple but delicious recipe for beef braised in Indian spices. Ground almonds are used to thicken the sauce, and yogurt may be added if you prefer a creamier result. I like to serve this as a weeknight dinner over fragrant basmati rice, accompanied by steamed green beans and warm naan, an Indian bread, which I buy at my neighborhood supermarket.

1 tbsp	vegetable oil	15 mL
2 lbs	stewing beef, trimmed and cut into 1-inch (2.5 cm) cubes	1 kg
2	onions, finely chopped	2
4	cloves garlic, minced	4
1 tsp	minced gingerroot	5 mL
1 to 2	long red or green chili peppers	1 to 2
2 tsp	ground cumin	10 mL
1 tsp	ground coriander	5 mL
1 tsp	turmeric	5 mL
1 tsp	salt	5 mL
1/2 tsp	cracked black peppercorns	2 mL
4	green or white cardamom pods	4
4	whole cloves	4
1/2 cup	beef stock or water	125 mL
1	bay leaf	1
1/4 cup	ground almonds	50 mL
1/2 cup	plain yogurt, optional	125 mL
	Hot cooked rice	

MAKE AHEAD
This dish can be partially prepared the night before it is cooked. Complete Step 2, heating 1 tbsp (15 mL) oil in pan before softening onions. Cover and refrigerate overnight. The next morning, brown beef (Step 1) or omit this step and place beef directly in slow cooker stoneware. Continue cooking as directed in Step 3.

1. In a skillet, heat oil over medium-high heat. Add beef, in batches, and brown. Using a slotted spoon, transfer to slow cooker stoneware.

2. Reduce heat to medium. Add onions and cook, stirring, until softened. Add garlic, gingerroot, chili pepper, cumin, coriander, turmeric, salt, peppercorns, cardamom and cloves and cook, stirring, for 1 minute. Add beef stock and bay leaf and bring to a boil.

3. Pour mixture over beef. Stir to combine. Cover and cook on **Low** for 8 to 10 hours or on **High** for 4 to 5 hours, until beef is tender. Stir in almonds, cover and cook on **High** for 10 minutes. Stir in yogurt, if using, and serve over hot cooked rice.

Cuban-Style Flank Steak

SERVES 6 TO 8

....

This is a traditional Cuban dish known as ropa vieja, *which is Spanish for "old clothes," so named because it was a way of using up leftover meat. In this version, flank steak is cooked and shredded, then cooked again in a spicy sauce. It is a great dish for the slow cooker as you can cook the meat overnight and, with a minimum of preparation, finish it off for dinner the following night. Serve the saucy meat over rice or use it as a filling for tortillas.*

Preliminary Cooking

1	flank steak, approximately 2 lbs (1 kg) (see Tips, page 78)	1
1	large onion, thinly sliced	1
6	cloves garlic, minced	6
1 tsp	dried oregano leaves	5 mL
½ tsp	salt	2 mL
8	cracked black peppercorns	8
1	bay leaf	1
2 tbsp	freshly squeezed lemon juice	25 mL
	Water or beef stock	

Second Cooking

2 tbsp	vegetable oil, divided	25 mL
8 oz	mushrooms, thinly sliced	250 g
2	onions, finely chopped	2
1 tsp	chili powder	5 mL
1 tsp	dried oregano leaves	5 mL
1	hot chili pepper, minced, optional	1
1 tsp	salt	5 mL
½ tsp	cracked black peppercorns	2 mL
1 tbsp	all-purpose flour	15 mL
1	each red and green bell pepper, roasted, peeled and cut into strips	1
2 cups	shredded Monterey Jack cheese, optional	500 mL
	Hot cooked rice or tortillas	

1. Place steak in slow cooker stoneware. Spread onion slices evenly over meat. Sprinkle garlic, oregano, salt, peppercorns and bay leaf over onions. Drizzle lemon juice over seasonings and add water to cover. Cover and cook on **Low** for 8 to 10 hours or on **High** for 4 to 5 hours, until meat is tender and shreds easily.

2. Allow meat to cool in cooking liquid. (If not proceeding to the second cooking immediately, cover and refrigerate meat and cooking liquid until ready to use.) Strain and reserve liquid. Using two forks, tear meat into shreds and transfer to slow cooker stoneware.

3. Second Cooking: In a skillet, heat 1 tbsp (15 mL) oil over medium-high heat. Add mushrooms and cook, stirring, until they lose their liquid. Transfer to slow cooker stoneware. Reduce heat to medium.

continued on page 78

4. Add remaining oil to pan. Add onions and cook, stirring, until softened. Add chili powder, oregano, chili pepper, if using, salt and peppercorns and cook, stirring, for 1 minute. Sprinkle flour over mixture and cook, stirring, for 1 minute. Add ½ cup (125 mL) reserved beef cooking liquid and cook, stirring, until thickened. Pour over beef and mushrooms and stir to combine. Lay pepper strips over top of mixture. Cover and cook on **Low** for 4 hours or on **High** for 2 hours, until mixture is hot and bubbly. Add cheese, if using.

5. Cover and cook on **High** for 10 minutes, until cheese is melted. Serve over hot cooked rice.

TIPS

• This is a great dish for those evenings when everyone is coming and going as you can leave the slow cooker on Warm and people can help themselves. Leave out tortillas and an assortment of garnishes, such as shredded lettuce, chopped red or green onion, shredded cheese, sour cream and salsa, for a family-friendly meal.

• You will need a large oval slow cooker to cook the steak in one piece. When placed in the slow cooker stoneware, the meat may extend up the sides a bit, but it will shrink as it cooks. If you are using a smaller slow cooker, cut the steak in half and proceed with the recipe.

Sussex-Style Steak with Mushrooms

SERVES 4 TO 6

....

This is a variation on an old English recipe, which I first came across in the late Elizabeth David's classic book Spices, Salt and Aromatics in the English Kitchen. *I had the great pleasure of meeting Elizabeth and having a very enjoyable lunch with her years ago in London, when I was writing an article on English food. She had a formidable knowledge of culinary history and cooking methodology and she was an inspirational writer on the joys of food. This dish, which takes barely five minutes to prepare, makes a delicious main course. Serve with mashed potatoes and green beans for a very tasty, traditional "meat and potatoes" meal.*

1	flank steak, approximately 2 lbs (1 kg) (see Tips, below)	1
	Salt and pepper to taste	
¼ cup	all-purpose flour	50 mL
1	small red onion, thinly sliced, or 8 green onions, white part only, thinly sliced	1
¼ cup	condensed beef broth, undiluted	50 mL
¼ cup	port wine, dark beer or additional condensed beef broth	50 mL
1 tbsp	olive oil	15 mL
3 or more	portobello mushrooms, stems removed (see Tips, below)	3 or more
2 tbsp	balsamic or red wine vinegar	25 mL
	Crumbled soft goat cheese, optional (see Tips, below)	

1. Season the meat and rub each side with an equal amount of flour. Place in bottom of slow cooker stoneware. Lay onions over top and pour in beef broth and port.

2. Brush mushrooms with olive oil and lay evenly over meat (they should cover the surface). Sprinkle with vinegar. Cover and cook on **Low** for 8 to 10 hours or on **High** for 4 to 5 hours.

3. When ready to serve, transfer steak with mushrooms to a deep platter. Stir in goat cheese, if using, and pour gravy over meat.

....

TIPS

• You will need a large oval slow cooker to cook the steak in one piece. When placed in the slow cooker stoneware, the meat may extend up the sides a bit, but it will shrink as it cooks. If you are using a smaller slow cooker, cut the steak in half and proceed with the recipe.

• The quantity of portobello mushrooms required for this recipe depends upon their size. You will want enough to cover the surface of the meat — as few as 3 large mushrooms or 5 or 6 smaller ones.

• The addition of goat cheese adds flavor and creaminess to the gravy; 1 to 2 oz (30 to 60 g) is sufficient for this recipe.

Beef and Sausage Chili

SERVES 8 TO 10

·······················

This is a hearty and flavorful chili. Serve with hot garlic bread and a tossed salad for a great meal.

MAKE AHEAD
This dish can be partially prepared the night before it is cooked. Complete Steps 1, 2 and 3. Cover and refrigerate meat and vegetable mixtures separately. The next day, continue cooking as directed in Step 4.

1 lb	Italian or chorizo sausage, removed from casings	500 g
1 lb	stewing beef, cut into ½-inch (1 cm) cubes	500 g
2	onions, finely chopped	2
4	cloves garlic, minced	4
2 tbsp	chili powder	25 mL
1 tbsp	dried oregano leaves	15 mL
1 tbsp	cumin seeds	15 mL
1 tsp	salt	5 mL
1 tsp	cracked black peppercorns	5 mL
2 to 3	jalapeño peppers, finely chopped	2 to 3
1	habanero pepper, minced (see Tips, page 82), optional	1
1	can (28 oz/796 mL) tomatoes, drained and chopped, ½ cup (125 mL) juice reserved	1
½ cup	condensed beef broth, undiluted	125 mL
1 tbsp	Worcestershire sauce	15 mL
2 cups	dried red kidney beans, cooked and drained, or 2 cans (19 oz/540 mL) red kidney beans, drained and rinsed	500 mL
2 cups	shredded Monterey Jack cheese	500 mL
	Finely chopped green onion or cilantro	

1. In a nonstick skillet, cook sausage over medium-high heat, breaking up with a wooden spoon, until no longer pink. Using a slotted spoon, transfer to slow cooker stoneware. Drain all but 1 tbsp (15 mL) fat from pan.

2. Add beef to pan, in batches, and cook until no longer pink. Transfer to slow cooker stoneware.

3. Reduce heat to medium. Add onions and cook, stirring, until softened. Add garlic, chili powder, oregano, cumin seeds, salt, peppercorns, jalapeño peppers and habanero pepper, if using, and cook, stirring, for 1 minute. Stir in tomatoes, reserved tomato juice, beef broth and Worcestershire sauce and bring to a boil.

continued on page 82

4. Pour mixture over meat. Add beans and stir well. Cover and cook on **Low** for 8 to 10 hours or on **High** for 4 to 5 hours, until beef is very tender. Add cheese and stir until melted. Ladle into bowls and garnish with green onions.

TIPS
• Since the spicing in sausage can vary dramatically, taste a bit after it is cooked and adjust the seasoning accordingly. (You may want to omit the habanero pepper, which is very hot.)
• If you are using a dried habanero pepper, be sure to soak it for 30 minutes in boiling water, before adding to recipe.
• Substitute 1 to 2 jalapeño peppers for the habanero pepper, if desired.

VARIATION
Hearty Beef Chili: For an all-beef version of this chili, substitute 1 lb (500 g) lean ground beef for the sausage.

PANTRY NOTES

Non-Standard Can Sizes
In today's global economy, it's not uncommon for food products, widely available in North American supermarkets, to be imported from distant locales and packaged or canned in non-standard sizes. Large cans of tomatoes come in 28 oz (796 mL) to 35 oz (980 mL) sizes. I've used the 28 oz (796 mL) size in all my recipes. If using a 35 oz (980 mL) can, drain off 1 cup (250 mL) liquid.

Blue Plate Chili

SERVES 4 TO 6

Here's a good, basic chili recipe — just like the chili my mother used to make or that we ate for lunch at local restaurants when, as a preschooler, I accompanied her on household errands. I have fond memories of those "blue plate specials" of chili and toast, and judging by my own family's response to this version, it remains a popular dish. I still serve it with toast — it wouldn't be the same without it.

MAKE AHEAD
This recipe may be partially prepared the night before it is cooked. Complete Steps 1 and 2, chilling cooked meat and onion mixture separately. Chop green pepper and cover. Refrigerate overnight. The next morning, combine meat with onion mixture and continue with Step 3.

1 tbsp	vegetable oil	15 mL
1 lb	lean ground beef	500 g
1	onion, finely chopped	1
3	stalks celery, peeled and thinly sliced	3
2	cloves garlic, minced	2
1 tbsp	chili powder	15 mL
1 tsp	caraway seeds	5 mL
1 tsp	salt	5 mL
1 tsp	cracked black peppercorns	5 mL
1	can (28 oz/796 mL) tomatoes, drained and coarsely chopped	1
½ cup	condensed beef broth, undiluted	125 mL
1	can (19 oz/540 mL) red kidney beans, drained and rinsed, or 1 cup (250 mL) dried red kidney beans, soaked, cooked and drained	1
1	green bell pepper, chopped	1

1. In a nonstick skillet, heat oil over medium-high heat. Add beef and cook, breaking up with a wooden spoon, until no longer pink. Using a slotted spoon, transfer to slow cooker stoneware.

2. Reduce heat to medium. Add onion and celery to pan and cook, stirring, until soft. Add garlic, chili powder, caraway seeds, salt and peppercorns and cook, stirring, for 1 minute. Stir in tomatoes and beef broth and bring to a boil. Transfer to slow cooker stoneware.

3. Stir in beans. Cover and cook on **Low** for 8 to 10 hours or on **High** for 4 to 5 hours. Increase heat to **High**. Add green pepper and cook for 20 minutes, until tender.

Chunky Black Bean Chili

Here is a great-tasting, stick-to-the-ribs chili that is perfect for a family dinner or casual evening with friends. The combination of milder New Mexico and ancho chili peppers gives the mix unique flavoring, and the optional fresh chili peppers will add heat. Serve with crusty country bread, a big green salad and robust red wine or ice cold beer.

3	dried ancho chili peppers	3
2	dried New Mexico chili peppers	2
1 tbsp	vegetable oil	15 mL
2 lbs	stewing beef, cut into 1-inch (2.5 cm) cubes	1 kg
2	onions, finely chopped	2
4	cloves garlic, minced	4
1 to 2	chili peppers, minced, optional (see Tip, below)	1 to 2
1 tbsp	cumin seeds	15 mL
1 tsp	cracked black peppercorns	5 mL
1 tsp	salt	5 mL
1	can (28 oz/796 mL) tomatoes, including juice	1
1½ cups	flat beer or beef stock	375 mL
2	cans (each 19 oz/540 mL) black beans, drained and rinsed, or 2 cups (500 mL) dried black beans, cooked and drained (see Basic Beans, page 214)	2
	Sour cream, optional	
	Finely chopped red or green onion, optional	
	Shredded Monterey Jack cheese, optional	
	Salsa, optional	

1. In a heatproof bowl, soak dried chilies in 4 cups (1 L) boiling water for 30 minutes. Drain and discard liquid. Remove stems, pat dry, chop finely and set aside.

2. In a nonstick skillet, heat oil over medium-high heat. Add beef, in batches, and brown. Using a slotted spoon, transfer to slow cooker stoneware. Reduce heat to medium.

3. Add onions and cook, stirring, until softened. Add garlic, chili peppers, if using, cumin seeds, peppercorns, salt and reserved chilies and cook, stirring, for 1 minute. Add tomatoes and cook, breaking up with the back of a spoon, until desired consistency is achieved. Add beer and bring to a boil.

4. Pour mixture over beef. Add beans and stir well. Cover and cook on **Low** for 8 to 10 hours or on **High** for 4 to 5 hours, until beef is very tender. To serve, ladle into bowls and top with your favorite garnishes.

TIP
• Almost any kind of fresh chili pepper will work in this recipe. Use habanero, jalapeño or long chili peppers, depending upon your preference.

MAKE AHEAD
This dish can be partially prepared ahead of time. Complete Steps 1 and 3, heating 1 tbsp (15 mL) oil in pan before softening the onions. Cover and refrigerate overnight. The next morning, brown the beef (Step 2), or if you're pressed for time, omit this step. Combine vegetable mixture, beef and beans in slow cooker stoneware. Continue cooking as directed in Step 4.

Polish Beef Stew with Sauerkraut and Sausage

SERVES 6

I can't think of a better way to conclude an active day in the chilly outdoors than to be greeted by a steaming plate of this robust stew. Serve with plenty of mashed potatoes to soak up the tasty sauce, and pass dark rye bread and sour cream at the table.

MAKE AHEAD
This dish can be partially prepared the night before it is cooked. Complete Steps 1 and 3. Cover and refrigerate overnight. The next morning, brown meat (Step 2), or if you're pressed for time, omit this step and place beef directly in slow cooker stoneware. Continue cooking as directed in Step 4.

4	slices bacon	4
2 lbs	stewing beef, cut into 1-inch (2.5 cm) cubes	1 kg
2	onions, finely chopped	2
4	cloves garlic, minced	4
1 tbsp	caraway seeds	15 mL
1 tsp	salt	5 mL
½ tsp	cracked black peppercorns	2 mL
4	juniper berries or 2 tbsp (25 mL) gin (see Tip, below)	4
1 tbsp	all-purpose flour	15 mL
1 cup	dry white wine	250 mL
½ cup	condensed beef broth, undiluted	125 mL
4 cups	sauerkraut, drained and rinsed	1 L
1 lb	kielbasa sausage, cut into ¼-inch (0.5 cm) slices	500 g
	Sour cream	

1. In a skillet, cook bacon over medium-high heat until crisp. Remove and drain thoroughly on paper towel. Crumble and refrigerate, covered, until ready to use. Drain all but 2 tbsp (25 mL) fat from pan.

2. Add beef, in batches, and brown. Using a slotted spoon, transfer to slow cooker stoneware.

3. Reduce heat to medium. Add onions and cook, stirring, until softened. Add garlic, caraway seeds, salt, peppercorns, juniper berries and reserved bacon. Cook, stirring, for 1 minute. Sprinkle flour over mixture and cook, stirring, for 1 minute. Add wine and beef broth, bring to a boil and cook, stirring, until mixture thickens. Stir in sauerkraut.

4. Add mixture to slow cooker stoneware. Stir to combine. Cover and cook on **Low** for 8 to 10 hours or on **High** for 4 to 5 hours, until beef is very tender. Stir in sausage. Cover and cook on **High** for 15 minutes, until sausage is heated through. Pass the sour cream.

TIP
• Juniper berries, which are harvested from evergreen shrubs, add a fresh, pine-like note to soups and stews. Juniper is the predominant aroma in gin, which makes the spirit an acceptable substitute in this stew, although the flavor will be much more muted than if the berries were used.

Mexican Meat Loaf

SERVES 6 TO 8

Here's a moist meat loaf with loads of flavor. The toppings, while not essential, lend a festive air to this comfort food classic. I like to serve this with mounds of steaming hot mashed potatoes or a seasoned rice.

¼ cup	long-grain white rice	50 mL
1 cup	boiling water	250 mL
2 lbs	lean ground beef	1 kg
2	onions, finely chopped	2
2	eggs, beaten	2
1 cup	tomato salsa	250 mL
1 cup	shredded Monterey Jack cheese	250 mL
1 tsp	chili powder	5 mL
1 tsp	dried oregano leaves	5 mL
1 tsp	ground cumin seeds	5 mL
1 tsp	salt	5 mL
½ tsp	cracked black peppercorns	2 mL
	Salsa, optional	
	Sour cream, optional	
	Finely chopped red or green onion, optional	

1. In a heatproof bowl, soak rice in boiling water for 30 minutes. Drain and discard liquid. Set aside.

2. Fold a 2-foot (60 cm) piece of foil in half lengthwise. Place on bottom and up sides of slow cooker stoneware.

3. In a large bowl, combine rice with remaining ingredients and mix well. Shape into a loaf and place in middle of foil strip on bottom of slow cooker stoneware. Cover and cook on **Low** for 8 to 10 hours or on **High** for 4 to 5 hours, until juices run clear when meat loaf is pierced with a fork or a meat thermometer reads 170°F (80°C). Lift out loaf using foil strip and transfer to a warm platter. Serve with additional salsa, sour cream and chopped red or green onion, if desired.

Mom's Meat Loaf

SERVES 6 TO 8

....

Here's a meat loaf that reminds me of the kind my mother used to make. Its simple, old-fashioned flavors are perfectly paired with a bubbling dish of scalloped potatoes or a big bowl of fluffy mashed potatoes to soak up the tasty juices.

2 lbs	lean ground beef	1 kg
1	can (10 oz/284 mL) condensed tomato soup	1
2	onions, finely chopped	2
2	stalks celery, peeled and finely diced	2
2	cloves garlic, minced	2
¼ cup	finely chopped flat-leaf parsley	50 mL
1 tsp	salt	5 mL
½ tsp	cracked black peppercorns	2 mL
3	eggs, lightly beaten	3
1½ cups	fine dry bread crumbs	375 mL

1. Fold a 2-foot (60 cm) piece of foil in half lengthwise. Place on bottom and up sides of slow cooker stoneware.

2. In a large bowl, combine ingredients and mix well. Shape into a loaf and place in middle of foil strip on bottom of slow cooker stoneware. Cover and cook on **Low** for 8 to 10 hours or on **High** for 4 to 5 hours, until juices run clear when meat loaf is pieced with a fork or a meat thermometer reads 170°F (80°C). Lift out loaf using foil strip and transfer to a warm platter. Pour juices into a sauceboat and serve alongside sliced loaf.

Short Ribs in Chili Sauce

SERVES 4 TO 6

Short ribs are one of my favorite cuts of meat, and this lively and delicious recipe takes these flavorful morsels in a satisfying southwesterly direction. To turn up the heat, add a habanero or Scotch bonnet pepper to the mouth-watering sauce. Serve with garlic mashed potatoes or Red Beans and Rice (see recipe, page 215).

MAKE AHEAD
This dish can be partially prepared the night before it is cooked. Complete Steps 1, 2 and 4. Cover and refrigerate overnight. The next morning, brown ribs (Step 3) and continue cooking as directed.

• *Preheat broiler*

1 tbsp	cumin seeds	15 mL
4	dried ancho chili peppers	4
½ to 1	habanero or Scotch bonnet pepper, optional (see Tips, below)	½ to 1
4 to 5 lbs	beef short ribs (see Tips, below)	2 to 2.5 kg
1 tsp	cracked black peppercorns	5 mL
4	cloves garlic	4
1 tsp	salt	5 mL
2 tbsp	freshly squeezed lemon juice	25 mL
2 cups	canned tomatoes, including juice	500 mL

1. In a skillet, toast cumin seeds over medium heat, stirring constantly, until they release their aroma and just begin to turn golden. Remove from heat and immediately transfer to a dish. In a spice grinder, with a pestle in a mortar or using a rolling pin, grind seeds. Set aside.

2. Return pan to element, add ancho chili peppers and dried habanero pepper, if using, and heat just until they release their aroma, about 30 seconds per side. Remove from heat and submerge peppers in 4 cups (1 L) boiling water. Soak for 30 minutes. Drain, discarding soaking liquid and stems. Pat dry.

3. Sprinkle ribs with peppercorns and brown under broiler, turning once, about 10 minutes per side. Transfer to a paper-towel-lined platter to drain.

4. In a food processor, combine garlic, salt, lemon juice, tomatoes and reserved chili peppers and cumin seeds. Process until mixture is smooth.

5. Cut short ribs into individual pieces and place in slow cooker stoneware. Pour sauce over top and stir to combine. Cover and cook on **Low** for 10 to 12 hours or on **High** for 5 to 6 hours, until ribs are tender and falling off the bone.

TIPS
• Either fresh or dried habanero or Scotch bonnet peppers work well in this sauce. If using a dried pepper, be sure to soak it along with the ancho chili peppers.
• Short ribs are a particularly delicious cut of beef, but they are very high in fat. Broiling them before adding to the slow cooker is essential to reduce fat.

Short Ribs with Orange Gremolata

SERVES 4 TO 6

These delicious Italian-inspired ribs are classy enough for the most discriminating guest yet homey enough for a family dinner. Serve with creamy polenta and steamed broccoli spears or rapini for a scrumptious Italian-themed meal.

MAKE AHEAD
This dish can be partially prepared the night before it is cooked. Complete Step 2. Cover and refrigerate overnight. The next morning, brown the ribs (Step 1) and continue cooking as directed.

• *Preheat broiler*

4 lbs	beef short ribs	2 kg
1 tbsp	vegetable oil	15 mL
2	onions, finely chopped	2
2	large carrots, peeled and thinly sliced	2
4	stalks celery, peeled and thinly sliced	4
4	cloves garlic, minced	4
1 tsp	salt	5 mL
1 tsp	cracked black peppercorns	5 mL
2	whole sprigs fresh thyme or ½ tsp (2 mL) dried thyme leaves	2
2 tbsp	all-purpose flour	25 mL
1 tbsp	tomato paste	15 mL
½ cup	condensed beef broth, undiluted	125 mL
½ cup	dry red wine	125 mL

Orange Gremolata

½ cup	flat-leaf parsley, finely chopped	125 mL
1	clove garlic, minced	1
	Zest of 1 orange, finely chopped	

1. Position broiler rack 6 inches (15 cm) from heat source. Broil ribs on both sides, turning once, until well browned, about 10 minutes per side. Drain on paper towels. Separate ribs if in strips and place in slow cooker.

2. In a skillet, heat oil over medium heat. Add onions, carrots and celery and cook, stirring, until softened. Add garlic, salt, peppercorns and thyme and cook, stirring, for 1 minute. Sprinkle flour over mixture and cook, stirring, for 1 minute. Add tomato paste, beef broth and wine and bring to a boil.

3. Pour mixture over ribs and stir to combine. Cover and cook on **Low** for 10 to 12 hours or on **High** for 5 to 6 hours, until ribs are tender and falling off the bone.

4. Orange Gremolata: Combine ingredients in a small bowl just before serving and pass at the table.

TIP
• Short ribs are juicy and succulent and blend well with many flavors. Their only drawback is that they are very fatty. Browning them under the broiler before cooking to render the fat is essential to success.

Short Ribs Braised in Spicy Black Bean Sauce

SERVES 4 TO 6

This terrific Chinese-inspired recipe for cooking short ribs is easy and so delicious you won't be able to resist seconds. I like to serve this with plain steamed rice and puréed spinach or Swiss chard (see Tips, below).

• *Preheat broiler*

4 to 5 lbs	beef short ribs	2 to 2.5 kg
¼ cup	finely chopped shallots	50 mL
1 tsp	minced gingerroot	5 mL
1 to 2	long red chili peppers, minced	1 to 2
3 tbsp	black bean sauce with garlic (see Tips, below)	45 mL
2 tbsp	sake or vodka	25 mL
½ tsp	cracked black peppercorns	2 mL
	Grated zest and juice of 1 orange	
	Finely chopped green onion	

1. Position broiler rack 6 inches (15 cm) from heat source. Broil ribs on both sides, turning once, until well browned, about 10 minutes per side. Drain on paper towels. Separate ribs if in strips and place in slow cooker.

2. In a bowl, combine remaining ingredients, except for green onion. Spoon over short ribs and toss to combine. Cover and cook on **Low** for 10 to 12 hours or on **High** for 5 to 6 hours, until ribs are tender and falling off the bone. Transfer to a warm platter and garnish with green onions.

TIPS
• If your guests like plenty of heat, use the second chili pepper; otherwise, stick with one.
• Black bean sauce with garlic is a prepared sauce that comes in a jar and is widely available. Look for it in the Asian foods section of supermarkets or in specialty stores.
• Serve this with puréed spinach or Swiss chard. For 1 lb (500 g) cooked spinach, use the white part of 2 green onions, half a clove of garlic, 1 tsp (5 mL) Dijon mustard, 2 tsp (10 mL) butter, and salt and freshly ground black pepper to taste. Combine in a food processor and process until smooth.

Veal Shanks with Lemon Sauce

SERVES 6 TO 8

Italy meets Greece in this delicious version of osso buco, which adds a Greek-inspired avgolemono sauce to the succulent braise. Be sure to set the table with coffee spoons so everyone will be able to enjoy the succulent marrow.

MAKE AHEAD

This dish can be partially prepared the night before it is cooked. Complete Step 2, adding 1 tbsp (15 mL) oil to pan before softening vegetables and sprinkling 2 tbsp (25 mL) flour over mixture before adding the wine. Cover and refrigerate overnight. The next day, brown the veal (Step 1) and continue with Steps 3 through 5.

6 to 8	sliced veal shanks	6 to 8
¼ cup	all-purpose flour	50 mL
2 tbsp	olive oil	25 mL
3	leeks, white part only, cleaned and thinly sliced (see Tip, page 203)	3
4	stalks celery, peeled and diced	4
2	carrots, peeled and diced	2
4	cloves garlic, minced	4
	Grated zest of 1 lemon, finely chopped	
1 tbsp	chopped fresh rosemary leaves	15 mL
1 tsp	salt	5 mL
½ tsp	cracked black peppercorns	2 mL
½ cup	dry white wine	125 mL
½ cup	condensed chicken broth, undiluted	125 mL
	Finely chopped fresh parsley	

Lemon Sauce

1	egg, separated	1
¼ cup	lemon juice	50 mL
1 cup	cooking juices from veal	250 mL

1. On a plate, coat veal shanks with flour, shaking off excess. Set any remaining flour aside. In a skillet, heat oil over medium heat. Add veal, in batches, and cook until lightly browned on all sides. Transfer to slow cooker stoneware.

2. Add leeks, celery and carrots to pan and cook, stirring, until vegetables are softened. Add garlic, lemon zest, rosemary, salt and peppercorns and cook, stirring, for 1 minute. Sprinkle reserved flour over mixture and cook, stirring, for 1 minute. Add wine and chicken broth and bring to a boil.

3. Pour mixture over veal, cover and cook on **Low** for 12 hours or on **High** for 6 hours, until veal is very tender.

4. Lemon Sauce: In a bowl, beat egg white until stiff. Beat in yolk, then gradually add lemon juice, beating constantly. Spoon off 1 cup (250 mL) cooking liquid from the veal and gradually beat into mixture.

5. To serve, arrange veal on a deep platter. Stir lemon mixture into cooking juices. Taste and adjust seasoning. Pour over veal. Garnish liberally with parsley.

Wine-Braised Veal with Rosemary

SERVES 6

This is a delicious Italian-inspired stew that is both simple and elegant. Serve over hot Slow-Cooked Polenta (see recipe, page 211) and accompany with steamed broccoli or rapini.

MAKE AHEAD
This dish can be partially prepared the night before it is cooked. Complete Steps 1 and 3, refrigerating cooked pancetta and vegetable mixtures separately. The next morning, add pancetta to vegetable mixture, place veal in slow cooker (don't bother with browning) and continue with Step 4.

1 tbsp	olive oil	15 mL
3 oz	pancetta or bacon, cut into 1/4-inch (0.5 cm) dice (see Tips, below)	90 g
2 lbs	stewing veal, cut into 1-inch (2.5 cm) cubes	1 kg
3	leeks, white part only, cleaned and coarsely chopped	3
3	large carrots, peeled and diced	3
2	stalks celery, peeled and diced	2
2	cloves garlic, minced	2
1 1/2 tbsp	chopped fresh rosemary leaves or dried rosemary leaves, crumbled (see Tips, below)	22 mL
1 tsp	salt	5 mL
1/2 tsp	cracked black peppercorns	2 mL
2 tbsp	all-purpose flour	25 mL
1/2 cup	dry red wine	125 mL
1/2 cup	condensed chicken broth, undiluted	125 mL
	Fresh rosemary sprigs, optional	

1. In a skillet, heat oil over medium heat. Add pancetta and cook, stirring, until browned. Using a slotted spoon, transfer to slow cooker stoneware.

2. Add veal to pan, in batches, and cook, stirring, just until it begins to brown. Using a slotted spoon, transfer to slow cooker stoneware.

3. Add leeks, carrots and celery to pan and cook, stirring, until softened. Add garlic, rosemary, salt and peppercorns and cook, stirring, for 1 minute. Sprinkle flour over mixture and cook, stirring, for 1 minute. Add wine and chicken broth and cook, stirring, until mixture thickens.

4. Pour mixture over meat and stir to combine. Cover and cook on **Low** for 8 to 10 hours or on **High** for 4 to 6 hours, until meat is tender. Garnish with rosemary sprigs, if using, and serve.

TIPS
• If you are using bacon in this recipe, be aware that the flavors will not be as pleasingly subtle. You will also need to drain all but 1 tbsp (15 mL) of the fat before proceeding with Step 2.
• If you are using fresh rosemary in this recipe and prefer a more pronounced rosemary flavor, bury a whole sprig of the herb in the meat before adding the sauce. Remove before serving.

Mexican-Style Veal Stew

SERVES 6

In this unusual but delicious stew, veal is braised in a little broth and mild vinegar to melt-in-your-mouth tenderness, then finished with fresh tomatoes, cilantro and crunchy almonds. An optional garnish of pimento-stuffed olives adds eye appeal. Serve over hot, fluffy rice and accompany with a green vegetable.

MAKE AHEAD
This dish can be partially prepared the night before it is cooked. Complete Steps 1 and 3, heating 1 tbsp (15 mL) oil in pan before softening onions. The next day, brown meat (Step 2), or if you're pressed for time, omit this step and add veal directly to slow cooker. Continue cooking as directed.

4	dried pasilla chili peppers (see Tip, right)	4
2 cups	boiling water	500 mL
1 tbsp	vegetable oil	15 mL
2 lbs	stewing veal, cut into 1-inch (2.5 cm) chunks	1 kg
2	onions, finely chopped	2
4	cloves garlic, minced	4
1 tsp	dried oregano leaves	5 mL
1 tsp	salt	5 mL
½ tsp	cracked black peppercorns	2 mL
6	whole cloves	6
1	cinnamon stick piece, about 2 inches (5 cm)	1
¼ cup	condensed chicken broth, undiluted	50 mL
2 tbsp	white wine vinegar	25 mL
2 tbsp	butter	25 mL
½ cup	whole blanched almonds	125 mL
6	sprigs cilantro	6
4	medium tomatoes, peeled and chopped	4
8	large pimento-stuffed green olives, sliced, optional	8
	Salt and freshly ground black pepper	

1. In a heatproof bowl, soak chilies in boiling water for 30 minutes. Drain and discard liquid. Pat dry with paper towel, chop finely and set aside.

2. In a nonstick skillet, heat oil over medium-high heat. Add veal, in batches, and brown. Transfer to slow cooker stoneware. Reduce heat to medium.

3. Add onions to pan and cook, stirring, until softened. Add garlic, oregano, salt, peppercorns, cloves and cinnamon stick and cook, stirring for 1 minute. Stir in chicken broth and vinegar and bring to a boil. Pour over veal. Cover and cook on **Low** for 8 hours or on **High** for 4 hours, until veal is tender.

4. In a skillet over medium heat, melt butter. Add almonds and cook, stirring, until browned. Transfer to food processor.

5. Add cilantro and tomatoes to pan and cook, stirring, for 1 minute. Season to taste with salt and pepper and transfer to food processor. Process with almonds until smooth. Stir into veal mixture. Discard cinnamon stick.

6. When ready to serve, transfer to a deep platter and garnish with olives, if desired.

TIP
• Pasilla chili peppers have a relatively mild flavor and a fruity taste, with slightly licorice overtones. They are usually available in supermarkets that carry the cellophane packages of dried chili peppers. If you can't find them, use an equal quantity of dried ancho or mulato chili peppers in this recipe.

PANTRY NOTES

Whole Leaf Herbs and Spices
For best results, use whole rather than ground herbs and spices in the slow cooker. Whole spices, such as cumin seeds and cracked black peppercorns, and whole leaf herbs, such as dried thyme and oregano leaves, release their flavors slowly throughout the long cooking period, unlike ground spices and herbs, which tend to lose flavor during slow cooking. If you're using fresh herbs, add them, finely chopped, during the last hour of cooking unless you include the whole stem (this works best with thyme and rosemary).

Pork and Lamb

Uptown Wieners and Beans

Uptown Wieners and Beans

SERVES 8

The year I graduated from university, I spent the summer in Munich, where my culinary education was broadened by two significant discoveries: well-made sauerkraut is delicious (nothing like the bottled variety I'd previously experienced); and the German people really do know a thing or two about sausages. There is a sausage for almost every occasion, and it is those tasty wursts — wiesswurst, brautwurst, knackwurst and numerous more esoteric varieties — that I had in mind when I developed this recipe. Of course, it works well with supermarket wieners, too.

2 cups	dried navy beans, soaked and cooked (see Basic Beans, page 214) or 2 cans (19 oz/540 mL) navy or great northern beans, drained and rinsed	500 mL
6	slices bacon, diced	6
2	onions, diced	2
2	cloves garlic, minced	2
1 cup	tomato ketchup	250 mL
2 tbsp	packed brown sugar	25 mL
2 tbsp	cider vinegar	25 mL
1 tbsp	grainy mustard	15 mL
1 tsp	salt	5 mL
1 tsp	cracked black peppercorns	5 mL
1 cup	apple cider or juice (approx.) (see Tips, below)	250 mL
1 cup	water (approx.)	250 mL
1 lb	good-quality wieners, cooked and cut into 1-inch (2.5 cm) pieces (see Tips, below)	500 g

1. In slow cooker stoneware, combine beans, bacon, onions and garlic.

2. In a small bowl, combine ketchup, brown sugar, vinegar, mustard, salt and peppercorns. Pour over bean mixture and stir to combine. Add apple juice and water in equal amounts, barely to cover. Cover and cook on **Low** for 10 to 12 hours or on **High** for 5 to 6 hours, until hot and bubbling. Add wieners, stir well, cover and cook on **High** for 30 minutes, until wieners are heated through and mixture is bubbling.

TIPS
- If you don't have apple cider or juice, use about 2 cups (500 mL) water.
- For best results, use freshly made sausage from a good butcher. Be sure to ask about the appropriate cooking method, as some wursts should be boiled, while others should be grilled or fried.

Pork and Black Bean Chili

Here's a festive and stick-to-your-ribs chili that is a perfect finish to a day in the chilly outdoors. I like to serve this with hot corn bread, a crisp green salad and a good Spanish rioja or ice cold beer. Olé!

MAKE AHEAD
This dish can be partially prepared the night before it is cooked. Complete Steps 1,2 and 4, heating 1 tbsp (15 mL) oil in pan before softening onions. The next morning, brown pork (Step 3), or if you're pressed for time, omit this step and place meat directly in slow cooker stoneware. Continue cooking as directed in Step 5.

2	dried ancho chili peppers	2
2 cups	boiling water	500 mL
1 tbsp	cumin seeds	15 mL
1 tbsp	vegetable oil	15 mL
2 lbs	pork shoulder, trimmed of excess fat and cut into 1-inch (2.5 cm) cubes	1 kg
2	onions, finely chopped	2
4	cloves garlic, minced	4
1 tbsp	dried oregano leaves	15 mL
1 tsp	salt	5 mL
½ tsp	cracked black peppercorns	2 mL
1	chipotle chili pepper in adobo sauce (see Pantry Notes, page 149)	1
2 tbsp	tomato paste	25 mL
½ cup	condensed chicken broth, undiluted	125 mL
1½ cups	flat beer	375 mL
2 cups	dried black beans, cooked and rinsed, or 2 cans (19 oz/540 mL) black beans, drained and rinsed	500 mL
	Sour cream, optional	
	Crushed tortilla chips, optional	
	Finely chopped red or green onion, optional	
	Finely chopped cilantro, optional	

1. In a heatproof bowl, soak chilies in boiling water for 30 minutes. Drain and discard liquid and stems. Pat dry and set aside.

2. In a dry skillet, toast cumin seeds over medium heat, stirring constantly, until they release their aroma and begin to brown. Immediately transfer to a small dish and set aside.

3. In a nonstick skillet, heat oil over medium-high heat. Add pork, in batches, and brown. Using a slotted spoon, transfer to slow cooker stoneware. Reduce heat to medium.

4. Add onions to pan and cook, stirring, until softened. Add garlic, oregano, salt, peppercorns, reserved cumin seeds and ancho peppers and cook, stirring, for 1 minute. Add chipotle pepper, tomato paste and chicken broth. Transfer contents of pan to a food processor and process until smooth.

5. Pour mixture over meat. Add beer and beans and stir to combine. Cover and cook on **Low** for 8 to 10 hours or on **High** for 4 to 5 hours, until pork is tender. Ladle into bowls and garnish with sour cream, crushed tortilla chips, chopped onion and cilantro.

Chili Verde

....

If you are tired of dark and brooding chilies, try this tasty alternative. It is robust yet lighter in look and feel than its beef and kidney bean relatives, and lends itself to colorful garnishes. Top with any combination of sour cream, chopped avocado sprinkled with lime juice, chopped tomato, shredded lettuce, finely chopped red onion, finely chopped cilantro and shredded Monterey Jack or Cheddar cheese for a delicious and nutritious meal.

2	dried ancho chili peppers or 2 fresh pasilla chilies	2
2 cups	boiling water	500 mL
1 tbsp	vegetable oil	15 mL
2 lbs	stewing pork, cut into 1-inch (2.5 cm) cubes	1 kg
3	onions, finely chopped	3
6	cloves garlic, minced	6
1	jalapeño pepper, finely chopped	1
1	habanero or Scotch bonnet chili pepper, finely chopped (see Tips, page 104), optional	1
1 tbsp	dried oregano leaves	15 mL
2 tsp	cumin seeds	10 mL
1 tsp	salt	5 mL
½ tsp	crushed black peppercorns	2 mL
3 cups	chicken stock	750 mL
2	cans (19 oz/540 mL) white kidney or great northern beans, drained and rinsed, or 2 cups (500 mL) dried white beans, cooked and drained (see Basic Beans, page 214)	2
1 tbsp	cider vinegar	15 mL
1	can (4.5 oz/127 mL) mild green chilies, chopped	1

MAKE AHEAD
This dish can be partially prepared the night before it is cooked. Complete Steps 1 and 3, heating 1 tbsp (15 mL) oil in pan before softening onions. Cover and refrigerate overnight. The next morning, brown pork (Step 2), or if you're pressed for time, omit this step and place meat directly in slow cooker stoneware. Continue cooking as directed in Step 4.

1. In a heatproof bowl, soak dried chilies in boiling water for 30 minutes, making certain that all parts of the pepper are submerged. Drain and discard liquid. Pat dry with paper towel, chop finely and set aside. If using fresh chilies, chop finely and set aside.

2. In a nonstick skillet, heat oil over medium-high heat. Add pork, in batches, and brown. Using a slotted spoon, transfer to slow cooker stoneware.

3. Reduce heat to medium. Add onions to pan and cook, stirring, until softened. Add garlic, jalapeño pepper, habanero pepper, if using, oregano, cumin seeds, salt, peppercorns and reserved chilies and cook, stirring, for 1 minute. Transfer mixture to food processor and process with 1 cup (250 mL) chicken stock until smooth.

continued on page 104

4. Add vegetable mixture to slow cooker stoneware along with remaining stock, beans and vinegar. Stir to combine. Cover and cook on **Low** for 8 to 10 hours or on **High** for 4 to 5 hours, until pork is tender. Stir in green chilies. Cover and cook on **High** until chilies are heated through and mixture is bubbling.

TIPS

• You can use a dried habanero pepper in this recipe, if desired. Just be sure to soak it for 30 minutes in boiling water before chopping and adding to the chili.

• If you prefer a thicker sauce, purée 1 cup (250 mL) of the beans before adding to the meat.

PANTRY NOTES

Dried Beans

Loaded with vitamins and fiber, dried beans are one of our most healthful edibles. But they can also be tough and flavorless, unless they are properly prepared. Since slow cookers were developed as an appliance for making baked beans, it's not surprising that most recipes featuring legumes execute very well in the slow cooker.

Pasta with Sausage and Lentils

SERVES 8 TO 10

Here's a rich and nutritious pasta sauce that will serve a crowd and have people coming back for seconds. It freezes well, so if you're cooking for fewer people, divide it up and freeze the unused portions.

MAKE AHEAD
This dish can be partially prepared the night before it is cooked. Complete Steps 1 and 2, chilling cooked sausage and tomato mixtures separately. Refrigerate overnight. The next morning, combine mixtures in slow cooker stoneware, add lentils and continue cooking as directed.

1 lb	Italian sausage, hot or mild, removed from casings	500 g
2	onions, finely chopped	2
2	large carrots, peeled, halved lengthwise and thinly sliced	2
2	stalks celery, peeled and thinly sliced	2
4	cloves garlic, minced	4
1 tsp	dried rosemary leaves	5 mL
4	whole cloves	4
1 tsp	salt	5 mL
½ tsp	cracked black peppercorns	2 mL
1	can (28 oz/796 mL) tomatoes, including juice, coarsely chopped	1
2 cups	chicken stock	500 mL
1 cup	dry red wine, water or additional broth	250 mL
2 cups	dried lentils, rinsed	500 mL
	Hot cooked pasta	
	Finely chopped parsley, optional	
	Freshly grated Parmesan cheese	

1. In a nonstick skillet, cook sausage over medium-high heat, breaking up with a spoon, until no longer pink. Using a slotted spoon, transfer to slow cooker stoneware. Drain all but 1 tbsp (15 mL) fat from pan. Reduce heat to medium.

2. Add onions, carrots and celery to pan and cook, stirring, until softened. Add garlic, rosemary, cloves, salt and peppercorns and cook, stirring, for 1 minute. Add tomatoes, chicken stock and wine and bring to a boil.

3. Pour mixture over sausage. Add lentils and stir to combine. Cover and cook on **Low** for 8 to 10 hours or on **High** for 4 to 5 hours.

4. Discard whole cloves. Place pasta in a large serving bowl. Spoon sauce over top and toss until well combined. Garnish with parsley, if using, and pass the Parmesan in a small bowl.

Santa Fe-Style Ribs

If you like Southwestern flavors, you'll love these ribs, which are seasoned with mild New Mexico chilies, toasted cumin seeds and roasted garlic. I recently served this recipe, with great success, as the centerpiece of a themed dinner for friends who were leaving for a vacation in Nevada. We began with Tortilla Soup and finished with Chocolate Flan with Toasted Almonds. To sustain the sensibility, I added a finely chopped jalapeño pepper and Monterey Jack cheese to the polenta, after stirring the cornmeal into the broth.

MAKE AHEAD
This dish can be partially prepared the night before it is cooked. Complete Steps 1, 3 and 4. Cover and refrigerate overnight. The next morning, broil ribs (Step 2) and complete Step 5.

• *Preheat broiler*

3	dried New Mexico chili peppers	3
2 cups	boiling water	500 mL
3½ to 4 lbs	country-style pork ribs (see Tip, page 108)	1.75 to 2 kg
1 tbsp	cumin seeds	15 mL
2 tbsp	vegetable oil	25 mL
8	cloves garlic, peeled	8
1 tsp	dried oregano leaves	5 mL
1 tsp	salt	5 mL
½ tsp	cracked black peppercorns	2 mL
1	can (28 oz/796 mL) tomatoes, drained and coarsely chopped	1
2 tbsp	white vinegar	25 mL

1. In a heatproof bowl, soak dried chilies in boiling water for 30 minutes. Drain, discarding soaking liquid and stems. Pat dry, chop finely and set aside.

2. Position broiler rack 6 inches (15 cm) from heat source. Broil ribs on both sides, until lightly browned, about 7 minutes per side. Drain on paper towels and transfer to slow cooker stoneware.

3. In a dry skillet, toast cumin seeds over medium heat, stirring constantly, until they release their aroma and begin to brown. Immediately transfer to a small dish and set aside.

4. Add oil to pan. Add garlic cloves and cook, stirring often, until golden and softened, being careful that the garlic doesn't burn. Add oregano, salt, peppercorns, reserved chilies and cumin seeds and cook, stirring, for 1 minute. Stir in tomatoes and vinegar and bring to a boil.

5. Pour sauce over ribs. Cover and cook on **Low** for 8 hours or on **High** for 4 hours, until ribs are tender and falling off the bone. Cut pork into individual ribs if a whole piece of meat was used and place on a deep platter. (If desired, spread a layer of polenta on platter first.) Cover with sauce and serve.

Italian-Style Ribs with Polenta

SERVES 6

Don't let the simplicity of this recipe fool you. Tender pork ribs are braised in a vegetable-based sauce, enhanced with wine and aromatic spices. The resulting sauce is rich-tasting but light, and the succulent ribs fall off the bone. I like to spoon the hot polenta over the bottom of a deep platter, lay the meat on top and pour the sauce over all. Garnish with additional sprigs of parsley for a presentation that looks as good as it tastes.

MAKE AHEAD
This dish can be partially prepared the night before it is cooked. Complete Step 2. Cover and refrigerate overnight. The next morning, broil ribs (Step 1) and complete Step 3.

• *Preheat broiler*

3½ to 4 lbs	country-style pork ribs (see Tip, below)	1.75 to 2 kg
1 tbsp	vegetable oil	15 mL
2	onions, minced	2
2	carrots, peeled and chopped	2
4	stalks celery, peeled and chopped	4
4	cloves garlic, minced	4
2 tsp	dried Italian seasoning	10 mL
1 tsp	salt	5 mL
½ tsp	cracked black peppercorns	2 mL
6	whole cloves	6
6	allspice berries	6
1	cinnamon stick piece, about 2 inches (5 cm)	1
1	can (28 oz/796 mL) tomatoes, drained and coarsely chopped	1
½ cup	dry red wine	125 mL
¼ cup	flat-leaf parsley, finely chopped	50 mL
	Slow-Cooked Polenta (see recipe, page 211)	

1. Position broiler rack 6 inches (15 cm) from heat source. Broil ribs on both sides, until lightly browned, about 7 minutes per side. Drain on paper towels and transfer to slow cooker stoneware.

2. In a nonstick skillet, heat oil over medium heat. Add onions, carrots and celery and cook, stirring, until softened. Add garlic, Italian seasoning, salt, peppercorns, cloves, allspice berries and cinnamon stick and cook, stirring, for 1 minute. Stir in tomatoes and red wine and bring to a boil.

3. Pour sauce over ribs. Cover and cook on **Low** for 8 hours or on **High** for 4 hours, until ribs are tender and falling off the bone. Discard cloves, allspice berries and cinnamon stick. Cut pork into individual ribs if a whole piece of meat was used. Garnish with parsley. Serve over hot polenta.

TIP
• This recipe works best if the ribs are in one big piece when cooked. (In my experience, this cut is usually only available from a butcher or in the pork roast section of the grocery store.) The single piece is easy to turn while broiling and will basically fall apart into individual servings after the meat is cooked.

Braised Pork with Mushrooms and Turnips

SERVES 6 TO 8

....

Pork and turnips, accentuated with garlic, is a marriage made in heaven. I like to serve this with crispy roasted potatoes and fresh green beans.

MAKE AHEAD
This dish can be partially prepared the night before it is cooked. Complete Steps 1 and 3, heating 1 tbsp (15 mL) oil in pan before softening vegetables. Cover and refrigerate mixture overnight. The next morning, heat 1 tbsp (15 mL) oil in skillet and brown roast (Step 2), or if you're pressed for time, omit this step and place roast directly in slow cooker stoneware and continue with Step 4.

1	package (½ oz/14 g) dried porcini mushrooms	1
1 cup	boiling water	250 mL
1 tbsp	vegetable oil	15 mL
2 lbs	boneless pork shoulder roast, trimmed of excess fat	1 kg
2	onions, finely chopped	2
3	carrots, peeled and thinly sliced	3
4	cloves garlic, minced	4
½ tsp	dried thyme leaves	2 mL
¼ tsp	ground allspice	1 mL
1 tsp	granulated sugar	5 mL
1 tsp	salt	5 mL
½ tsp	cracked black peppercorns	2 mL
2 tbsp	all-purpose flour	25 mL
½ cup	dry white wine, water or chicken stock	125 mL
3 cups	peeled and diced yellow turnip	750 mL

1. In a heatproof bowl, soak mushrooms in boiling water for 30 minutes. Strain through a fine sieve, reserving liquid. Pat mushrooms dry and chop finely. Set aside.

2. In a nonstick skillet, heat oil over medium-high heat. Add pork, in batches, and brown on all sides. Transfer to slow cooker stoneware.

3. Reduce heat to medium. Add onions and carrots to pan and cook, stirring, until softened. Add garlic, thyme, allspice, sugar, salt, peppercorns and reserved mushrooms and cook, stirring, for 1 minute. Sprinkle flour over mixture and cook, stirring, for 1 minute. Add reserved mushroom liquid and wine and cook, stirring, until mixture thickens. Stir in turnips.

4. Pour mixture over pork. Cover and cook on **Low** for 8 to 10 hours or on **High** for 4 to 5 hours, until meat is very tender. To serve, cut meat into serving-size pieces, place on a deep platter and cover with turnips and sauce.

Saucy Pork Chops with Cranberries

SERVE 4 TO 6

More than any other meat, pork has a great affinity for fruit. Here's a delicious recipe that combines cranberries and marmalade in a sauce that is easy enough for weeknight dinners but so tasty you may want to serve it for special occasions.

1 tbsp	vegetable oil	15 mL
4 to 6	loin pork chops, 1 inch (2.5 cm) thick (see Tip, below)	4 to 6
2	leeks, white part only, cleaned and thinly sliced (see Tip, page 203)	2
2	cloves garlic, minced	2
1 tsp	salt	5 mL
½ tsp	cracked black peppercorns	2 mL
½ cup	port wine, Madeira or orange juice	125 mL
¼ cup	orange marmalade	50 mL
½ cup	dried cranberries	125 mL

1. In a nonstick skillet, heat oil over medium-high heat. Brown pork chops on both sides, in batches, and transfer to slow cooker stoneware. Drain fat from pan.

2. Reduce heat to medium. Add leeks and cook, stirring, until softened. Add garlic, salt and peppercorns and cook, stirring, for 1 minute. Stir in port, marmalade and cranberries and bring to a boil.

3. Pour mixture over pork. Cover and cook on **Low** for 5 hours or on **High** for 2½ hours, until pork is tender and just a hint of pink remains. Transfer to a warm platter and serve immediately.

TIP
• You can use pork shoulder butt chops in this recipe, but increase cooking time to 8 to 10 hours on **Low** or 4 to 5 hours on **High**.

VARIATION
Roast Pork with Cranberry Sauce: Substitute 1 boneless pork shoulder butt roast (about 3 lbs/1.5 kg), trimmed of fat, for the pork chops. Brown the roast on all sides (Step 1), then proceed as directed. Increase the cooking time to 10 hours on **Low** or 5 hours on **High**, until pork is very tender.

Hot Pot Pork Chops

·····································

Here's an easy-to-make Chinese-inspired dish that demonstrates how the use of fruit and prepared sauces, which are readily available at supermarkets, can add zest to the simplest recipes. Serve this over fluffy white rice for a great weeknight meal.

MAKE AHEAD
This dish can be partially prepared the night before it is cooked. Complete Step 2, heating 1 tbsp (15 mL) oil in pan before adding garlic. The next day, brown the pork (Step 1) and continue cooking as directed in Step 3.

1 tbsp	vegetable oil	15 mL
4 to 6	loin pork chops, 1 inch (2.5 cm) thick (see Tips, below)	4 to 6
4	cloves garlic, minced	4
1 tsp	minced gingerroot	5 mL
1	long red or green chili pepper, finely chopped (see Tips, below)	1
½ tsp	cracked black peppercorns	2 mL
	Grated zest and juice of 1 orange	
2 tbsp	soy sauce	25 mL
1 tbsp	hoisin sauce	15 mL
1 tbsp	cornstarch, dissolved in 2 tbsp (25 mL) water	15 mL
	Finely chopped green onions, optional	

1. In a nonstick skillet, heat oil over medium-high heat. Brown pork chops on both sides, in batches if necessary, and transfer to slow cooker stoneware. Drain fat from pan.

2. Reduce heat to medium. Add garlic, gingerroot, chili pepper and peppercorns to skillet and cook, stirring, for 1 minute. Add orange zest and juice, soy sauce and hoisin sauce and bring to a boil.

3. Pour mixture over pork chops. Cover and cook on **Low** for 4 to 5 hours or on **High** for 2 to 2½ hours, until pork is tender and just a hint of pink remains. Remove pork chops from slow cooker and place on a platter. Pour cooking liquid into a saucepan and bring to a boil. Add cornstarch mixture and stir until thickened. Pour over pork, garnish with green onions, if desired, and serve piping hot.

·····································

TIPS
• You can use pork shoulder butt chops in this recipe, but increase cooking time to 8 to 10 hours on **Low** or 4 to 5 hours on **High**.
• If you don't have fresh chili peppers, stir in a bottled Asian chili pepper sauce such as Sambal Oelek to taste, after sauce has been thickened with cornstarch.

Mom's Smothered Pork Chops

SERVES 4 TO 6

There are few recipes that remind me more of growing up than this one. I loved returning home from school to be greeted by the delicious aroma wafting through the house. Feel free to vary the cut of pork you use in this recipe. The sauce is equally good on loin chops or country-style ribs (see Tip, below). Serve with plenty of hot mashed potatoes to soak up the sauce.

¼ cup	all-purpose flour	50 mL
½ tsp	salt	2 mL
¼ tsp	freshly ground black pepper	1 mL
4 to 6	pork shoulder butt chops, about 2 to 3 lbs (1 to 1.5 kg)	4 to 6
2 tbsp	vegetable oil	25 mL
2	onions, finely chopped	2
2	cloves garlic, minced	2
½ cup	tomato-based chili sauce	125 mL
2 tbsp	cider vinegar	25 mL
2 tbsp	packed brown sugar	25 mL
1 tbsp	Worcestershire sauce	15 mL
1 tsp	dry mustard	5 mL

1. On a plate, combine flour, salt and black pepper. Dredge pork in mixture, coating both sides.

2. In a nonstick skillet, heat oil over medium heat. Add pork, in batches, and brown on both sides. Transfer to slow cooker stoneware.

3. Add onions to pan, adding more oil if necessary, and cook, stirring, until softened. Add garlic and cook, stirring, for 1 minute. Stir in chili sauce, vinegar, brown sugar, Worcestershire sauce and mustard. Bring to a boil.

4. Pour sauce over pork. Cover and cook on **Low** for 8 hours or on **High** for 4 hours, until meat is tender.

TIP
• If using loin cut pork chops, make sure they are about 1 inch (2.5 cm) thick and reduce cooking time to 4 to 5 hours on **Low** or 2 to 2½ hours on **High**.

VARIATION
Smothered Ribs: Substitute 3½ to 4 lbs (1.75 to 2 kg) country-style ribs for the pork chops. Broil the ribs for 5 minutes per side, then place in slow cooker stoneware. Heat 1 tbsp (15 mL) oil in skillet and proceed with Steps 3 and 4.

MAKE AHEAD
This dish can be partially prepared the night before it is cooked. Complete Step 3, heating 1 tbsp (15 mL) oil in pan before softening onions. Cover and refrigerate overnight. The next morning, complete Steps 1, 2 and 4.

Southwestern Shepherd's Pie

SERVES 6 TO 8

....

Here's a New World twist on a traditional English favorite. Pork, rather than traditional ground beef, is cooked in a robust Southwestern-flavored sauce and covered with a sweet potato topping. Add a salad or a steamed green vegetable and crusty rolls for a delicious and distinctive meal.

MAKE AHEAD
This dish can be partially prepared the night before it is cooked. Complete Steps 1 and 3, heating 1 tbsp (15 mL) oil in pan before softening onions. Cover and refrigerate. Make topping, cover and refrigerate. The next morning, brown pork (Step 2), or if you're pressed for time, omit this step and add pork to onion mixture in slow cooker stoneware and continue with Step 5.

2	dried New Mexico chili peppers	2
2 cups	boiling water	500 mL
1 tbsp	vegetable oil	15 mL
2 lbs	stewing pork, cut into 1-inch (2.5 cm) cubes	1 kg
2	onions, finely chopped	2
4	cloves garlic, minced	4
1 to 2	jalapeño peppers, finely chopped	1 to 2
2 tsp	cumin seeds	10 mL
1 tsp	dried oregano leaves	5 mL
1 tsp	ground cinnamon	5 mL
½ tsp	ground allspice	2 mL
1 tsp	salt	5 mL
½ tsp	cracked black peppercorns	2 mL
1 tsp	grated lime zest	5 mL
½ cup	lime juice	125 mL

Sweet Potato Topping

4	medium sweet potatoes, cooked and mashed	4
2 tbsp	butter	25 mL
1 tbsp	packed brown sugar	15 mL
	Salt and freshly ground black pepper	

1. In a heatproof bowl, soak New Mexico chilies in boiling water for 30 minutes. Drain, discarding soaking liquid and stems. Pat dry, chop finely and set aside.

2. In a nonstick skillet, heat oil over medium-high heat. Add pork, in batches, and brown on all sides. Using a slotted spoon, transfer to slow cooker stoneware.

3. Reduce heat to medium. Add onions to pan and cook, stirring, until softened. Add garlic, jalapeño peppers, cumin seeds, oregano, cinnamon, allspice, salt, peppercorns and reserved New Mexico chilies and cook, stirring, for 1 minute. Stir in lime zest and juice. Pour mixture over pork and stir to combine.

4. Sweet Potato Topping: In a bowl, mix together sweet potatoes, butter and brown sugar until well combined. Season to taste.

5. Spread topping over pork mixture. Cover and cook on **Low** for 8 hours or on **High** for 4 hours, until pork is tender and mixture is hot and bubbling.

Pozole

Pozole is a Mexican dish traditionally served at Christmas, often as a soup. Its key ingredient is hominy, a kind of processed corn with a distinctive, smoky taste. Pass small bowls filled with traditional Mexican garnishes, such as shredded lettuce and chopped radishes, as well as chopped onion and cilantro and lime wedges. Accompanied with a green salad and warm tortillas, it's a great meal — perfect for a casual evening with friends.

2	dried ancho chili peppers	2
2 cups	boiling water	500 mL
4	slices bacon	4
2 lbs	pork shoulder, trimmed of excess fat and cut into 1-inch (2.5 cm) cubes	1 kg
2	onions, finely chopped	2
4	cloves garlic, minced	4
1 tbsp	dried oregano leaves	15 mL
1 tbsp	cumin seeds	15 mL
1 tsp	salt	5 mL
½ tsp	cracked black peppercorns	2 mL
2 tsp	grated lime zest	10 mL
2 tbsp	lime juice	25 mL
1 cup	chopped tomatoes (see Tips, right)	250 mL
1	can (10 oz/284 mL) condensed chicken broth, undiluted	1
1	can (29 oz/824 mL) hominy, drained and rinsed (see Tips, right)	1
2	green bell peppers, chopped	2
	Shredded lettuce, optional	
	Chopped radish, optional	
	Chopped red or green onion, optional	
	Finely chopped cilantro, optional	
	Lime wedges, optional	

MAKE AHEAD
This dish can be partially prepared the night before it is cooked. Complete Steps 1, 2 and 4. Cover and refrigerate onion mixture. The next morning, heat 1 tbsp (15 mL) oil in pan and brown the pork, or if you're pressed for time, omit this step and continue as directed.

1. In a heatproof bowl, soak ancho chili peppers in boiling water for 30 minutes. Drain and discard soaking liquid and stems. Set aside.

2. In a skillet, cook bacon over medium-high heat, until crisp. Drain on paper towel and crumble. Cover and refrigerate until ready to use. Drain all but 2 tbsp (25 mL) fat from pan.

3. Add pork, in batches, and brown. Using a slotted spoon, transfer to slow cooker stoneware. Reduce heat to medium.

4. Add onions to pan and cook, stirring, until softened. Add garlic, oregano, cumin seeds, salt, peppercorns and reserved ancho chili peppers and cook, stirring, for 1 minute.

5. Transfer mixture to a food processor. Add lime zest and juice and tomatoes and process until smooth. Add chicken broth and pulse to combine.

6. Pour mixture over pork. Stir in hominy. Cover and cook on **Low** for 8 to 10 hours or on **High** for 4 to 5 hours, until pork is tender. Stir in reserved bacon and green bell peppers. Cover and cook on **High** for 20 minutes, until peppers are tender.

TIPS
• Hominy is available in food stores catering to a Latin American clientele and in many supermarkets, particularly in the southern United States.
• If using canned tomatoes, drain before measuring.

VARIATION
Pork and Chickpea Stew: Substitute 2 cups (500 mL) dried chickpeas, cooked and drained (see Basic Beans, page 214), or 2 cans (19 oz/540 mL) chickpeas, drained and rinsed, for the hominy.

PANTRY NOTES

Ancho Chili Peppers
Although fresh chili peppers add heat and many different tastes, dried chilies actually have more intense and complex flavors. Ancho chili peppers, which are dried poblano chilies, are among the most versatile. Large and wide at the top, tapering to a point, they are purplish in color. Relatively mild in terms of heat, they have a fruity, slightly smoky flavor, with hints of coffee, tobacco and raisin. They are used extensively in Mexican cooking.

Sausage and Barley Jambalaya

SERVES 6

As this recipe demonstrates, barley is more than an ingredient to be added to the soup pot. A dense and chewy grain, barley is both nutritious and satisfying. It's a great comfort food, and I'm always looking for ways to include it in family meals. This flavorful mixture makes a great weeknight dinner or a terrific dish for a Friday night potluck with friends. Add a tossed salad, crusty country-style bread, some robust wine and enjoy.

MAKE AHEAD
This dish can be partially prepared the night before it is cooked. Complete Steps 1 and 2, chilling the cooked sausage and tomato barley mixtures separately. Refrigerate overnight. The next morning, continue with Step 3.

1 lb	hot or mild Italian sausage, removed from casings	500 g
2	onions, finely chopped	2
2	cloves garlic, minced	2
1	long red chili or jalapeño pepper, finely chopped	1
2 tsp	Cajun seasoning (see Tips, below)	10 mL
1 tsp	dried oregano leaves	5 mL
1 tsp	salt	5 mL
½ tsp	cracked black peppercorns	2 mL
1 cup	pearl barley, thoroughly rinsed under cold running water	250 mL
1	can (28 oz/796 mL) tomatoes, including juice, coarsely chopped	1
3 cups	chicken stock	750 mL
8 oz	medium shrimp, cooked, peeled and deveined (see Step 3, page 164)	250 g
1	roasted red pepper, finely chopped (see Tips, page 24)	1

1. In a nonstick skillet, cook sausage over medium-high heat, breaking up with a spoon, until no longer pink. Using a slotted spoon, transfer to slow cooker stoneware. Drain all but 1 tbsp (15 mL) fat from pan. Reduce heat to medium.

2. Add onions to pan and cook, stirring, until softened. Add garlic, chili pepper, Cajun seasoning, oregano, salt and peppercorns and cook, stirring, for 1 minute. Add barley and stir well. Add tomatoes and chicken stock and bring to a boil.

3. Pour mixture over sausage and stir. Cover and cook on **Low** for 6 to 8 hours or on **High** for 3 to 4 hours. Add shrimp and roasted pepper. Cover and cook on **High** for 20 minutes, until shrimp is heated through.

TIPS
• If you don't have a fresh chili pepper, stir in hot pepper sauce to taste, after the jambalaya is cooked.
• Cajun seasoning is available in many supermarkets and specialty food stores. If you can't find it, substitute 1 tsp (5 mL) each dried thyme leaves and paprika to this recipe.

Cassoulet

SERVES 12

Years ago, before I became a parent, I often spent long periods of time in the kitchen preparing elaborate meals. In those days, one of my signature dishes was a cassoulet that took several days to prepare. Many friends remember it fondly, and when they heard I was writing a slow cooker cookbook, they urged me to include the recipe. The truth is, I simply don't have time to cook like that any more. So here is a pared-down version of that comfort food classic. It's still delicious and ideal for serving a crowd or as the centerpiece of a buffet party.

MAKE AHEAD
This dish can be partially prepared the night before it is cooked. Complete Steps 1 and 2, cooking beans overnight. Cover and refrigerate overnight. The next morning, continue cooking as directed.

• *Large (minimum 6 quart) slow cooker*

1	smoked ham hock	1
2 cups	dried white navy beans, soaked, drained and rinsed	500 mL
1 tbsp	vegetable oil	15 mL
2	onions, finely chopped	2
2	carrots, peeled and diced	2
2	stalks celery, peeled and diced	2
1	sprig fresh rosemary or 2 tsp (10 mL) dried rosemary leaves	1
4 cups	chicken stock or water (approx.)	1 L
1 tbsp	salt	15 mL
4	cloves garlic, put through a press	4
½ tsp	cracked black peppercorns	2 mL
½ tsp	dried thyme leaves	2 mL
2 lbs	boneless pork shoulder, trimmed of fat and cut into 4 pieces	1 kg
⅛ tsp	each ground cinnamon, allspice and cloves	0.5 mL
1	lamb shank (about 1 lb/500 g), cut into 4 pieces	1
2 tbsp	tomato paste	25 mL
2	bay leaves	2
1 lb	kielbasa, cut into ¼-inch (0.5 cm) slices	500 g

Bread Crumb Topping

2 cups	fresh bread crumbs	500 mL
½ cup	finely chopped fresh parsley	125 mL
¼ cup	melted butter	50 mL

1. In slow cooker stoneware, combine ham hock and beans. In a skillet, heat oil over medium heat. Add onions, carrots and celery and cook, stirring, until softened. Add rosemary and cook, stirring, for 1 minute. Transfer mixture to slow cooker stoneware. Add chicken stock to cover beans. Cover and cook on **Low** for 10 to 12 hours, until beans are tender.

2. In a bowl, combine salt, garlic, peppercorns and thyme. Rub mixture into pork. Place pork in a bowl, cover and refrigerate overnight.

3. Preheat oven to 350°F (180°C). On a plate, combine cinnamon, allspice and cloves. Roll lamb shanks in mixture and place, narrow end up, on a broiling pan. Scrape excess salt from pork shoulder and place on same broiling pan. Roast in preheated oven for 1 hour.

4. Remove ham hock from beans. Remove tough skin and shred meat. Discard skin and bone. Cover and refrigerate meat. Stir tomato paste and bay leaves into bean mixture.

5. Cut roasted pork into 1-inch (2.5 cm) squares and add along with lamb shanks to bean mixture. Stir to combine. Cover and cook on **Low** for 8 hours or on **High** for 4 hours. Remove lamb shanks from mixture and scrape meat from bones. Discard bones and return meat to beans. Stir in kielbasa and reserved meat from ham hock (see Tips, below). Transfer mixture to baking dishes, if necessary.

6. Bread Crumb Topping: Preheat oven to 350°F (180°C). In a bowl, combine ingredients. Sprinkle over cassoulet and bake, uncovered, for 1 hour.

TIPS
• Using the slow cooker to make cassoulet makes it a manageable project. Cook the beans and marinate the pork overnight (Steps 1 and 2). The next morning, continue cooking as directed.
• This is a large quantity of cassoulet, and when the sausage and ham meat is added, it may not fit comfortably in the slow cooker stoneware. I have a gargantuan baking dish, Mexican in origin, that I use for the final assembly. You may need to transfer the bean mixture to two large baking dishes before adding the bread crumb topping. If you are serving this as a dinner dish and have enough pottery, consider spooning the cassoulet into individual-serving-size ovenproof tureens. Add the topping and bake as directed.

Curried Lamb with Apricots

SERVES 6

This tasty curry, speckled with apricots, looks as good as it tastes. I like to serve this over hot white rice, with a dish of mango chutney on the side to complement and intensify the flavor of the fruit.

MAKE AHEAD
This dish can be partially prepared the night before it is cooked. Complete Step 2, heating 1 tbsp (15 mL) oil in pan before softening onions. Cover and refrigerate overnight. The next morning, brown lamb (Step 1), or if you're pressed for time, omit this step and add meat directly to slow cooker stoneware. Continue cooking as directed in Step 3.

1 tbsp	vegetable oil	15 mL
2 lbs	stewing lamb, cut into 1-inch (2.5 cm) cubes	1 kg
2	onions, finely chopped	2
4	cloves garlic, minced	4
1 to 2	long green chili peppers, finely chopped	1 to 2
1 tsp	minced gingerroot	5 mL
4	white or green cardamom pods	4
1	cinnamon stick piece, about 2 inches (5 cm)	1
1 tsp	turmeric	5 mL
1 tsp	ground cumin seeds	5 mL
1 tsp	ground coriander seeds	5 mL
1 tsp	salt	5 mL
½ tsp	cracked black peppercorns	2 mL
½ cup	beef stock	125 mL
1½ cups	dried apricots, cut in half	375 mL
	Finely chopped parsley or cilantro, optional	
	Cooked white rice	
	Mango chutney, optional	

1. In a nonstick skillet, heat oil over medium-high heat. Add lamb, in batches, and brown. Transfer to slow cooker stoneware.

2. Reduce heat to medium. Add onions to pan and cook, stirring, until softened. Add garlic, chili pepper, gingerroot, cardamom, cinnamon stick, turmeric, cumin seeds, coriander seeds, salt and peppercorns and cook, stirring, for 1 minute, until spices release their aroma. Stir in beef stock.

3. Pour mixture over lamb. Cover and cook on **Low** for 8 to 10 hours or on **High** 4 to 5 hours, until lamb is very tender. Stir in apricots. Cover and cook on **High** for 20 minutes, until fruit is heated through. Garnish with parsley, if using. Discard cinnamon stick. Serve over hot white rice and pass the chutney, if using.

Irish Stew

This hearty and delicious stew is an old favorite that really can't be improved upon. All it needs is a green vegetable such as string beans or broccoli, crusty rolls or a loaf of country-style bread, and a big glass of Guinness or a robust red wine.

MAKE AHEAD
This recipe can be partially prepared the night before it is cooked. Complete Step 3, heating 1 tbsp (15 mL) oil in pan before softening vegetables. Cover and refrigerate overnight. The next morning, brown lamb (Steps 1 and 2) and complete Step 4.

¼ cup	all-purpose flour	50 mL
1 tsp	salt	5 mL
½ tsp	cracked black peppercorns	2 mL
¼ cup	vegetable oil	50 mL
2 lbs	stewing lamb, cut into 1-inch (2.5 cm) cubes	1 kg
3	onions, finely chopped	3
2	large carrots, peeled and diced	2
1 tsp	dried thyme leaves	5 mL
2 tbsp	tomato paste	25 mL
1 tbsp	Worcestershire sauce	15 mL
1 cup	beef stock	250 mL
4	medium potatoes, peeled and cut into ½-inch (1 cm) cubes	4
1½ cups	green peas	375 mL

1. On a plate, combine flour, salt and peppercorns. Lightly coat lamb with mixture, shaking off the excess. Set any remaining flour mixture aside.

2. In a skillet, heat oil over medium-high heat. Add lamb, in batches, and brown. Transfer to slow cooker stoneware. Reduce heat to medium. Drain all but 1 tbsp (15 mL) fat from pan.

3. Add onions and carrots to pan and cook, stirring, until softened. Add thyme and reserved flour mixture and cook, stirring, for 1 minute. Stir in tomato paste, Worcestershire sauce and beef stock and bring to a boil.

4. Place potatoes in slow cooker stoneware. Add onion mixture and stir to combine. Cover and cook on **Low** for 10 hours or on **High** for 5 hours, until mixture is bubbling and lamb is tender. Stir in peas. Cover and cook on **High** for 15 to 20 minutes.

Lamb Shanks Braised in Guinness

This Irish-inspired combination is a classic. Add a green vegetable and mounds of mashed potatoes, sprinkled with finely chopped green onion, to soak up the delicious sauce.

¼ cup	all-purpose flour	50 mL
1 tsp	salt	5 mL
½ tsp	cracked black peppercorns	2 mL
4 lbs	lamb shanks, whole or sliced (see Tip, below)	2 kg
2 tbsp	vegetable oil	25 mL
4	onions, finely chopped	4
4	cloves garlic, minced	4
1 tsp	dried thyme leaves	5 mL
2 tbsp	tomato paste	25 mL
1½ cups	Guinness or other dark beer	375 mL
½ cup	condensed beef broth, undiluted	125 mL

1. On a plate, combine flour, salt and peppercorns. Lightly coat lamb shanks with mixture, shaking off the excess. Set any remaining flour mixture aside.

2. In a skillet, heat oil over medium-high heat. Add lamb, in batches, and cook, turning, until lightly browned. Transfer to slow cooker stoneware.

3. Reduce heat to medium. Add onions to pan and cook, stirring, until softened. Add garlic and thyme and reserved flour mixture and cook, stirring, for 1 minute. Stir in tomato paste, beer and broth and cook, stirring, until mixture thickens. Pour over meat. Cover and cook on **Low** for 10 to 12 hours or on **High** for 5 to 6 hours, until meat is falling off the bone.

TIP
• Whether you cook the lamb shanks whole or have them cut into pieces is a matter of preference. However, if the shanks are left whole, you will be able to serve only four people — each will receive one large shank.

Braised Lamb Shanks with Luscious Legumes

SERVES 6 TO 8

Lamb cooked with legumes in a flavorful wine-based sauce is a French tradition. No wonder — it is a mouth-watering combination. Serve this with crusty bread, a green salad or garden-fresh tomatoes in vinaigrette, and a robust red wine for a memorable meal. For a change, try making this recipe using chickpeas instead of beans.

MAKE AHEAD
This dish can be partially prepared the night before it is cooked. Place beans in water. Complete Step 4, heating 1 tbsp (15 mL) oil in pan before softening vegetables. Cover and refrigerate overnight. The next morning, complete remaining steps.

2 cups	dried white navy beans or flageolets, soaked, rinsed and drained (see Tips, below)	500 mL
¼ cup	all-purpose flour	50 mL
1 tsp	salt	5 mL
½ tsp	cracked black peppercorns	2 mL
6	lamb shanks, whole or sliced	6
¼ cup	vegetable oil	50 mL
2	onions, finely chopped	2
2	carrots, peeled and diced	2
4	stalks celery, peeled and diced	4
6	cloves garlic, minced	6
1 tbsp	finely chopped rosemary	15 mL
	Grated zest and juice of 1 orange	
1 cup	condensed beef broth, undiluted	250 mL
½ cup	dry red wine	125 mL
	Finely chopped fresh parsley	

1. Place beans in slow cooker stoneware.

2. On a plate, combine flour, salt and peppercorns. Lightly coat lamb shanks with mixture, shaking off the excess. Set any remaining flour mixture aside.

3. In a skillet, heat oil over medium-high heat. Add lamb, in batches, and cook until lightly browned on all sides. Transfer to slow cooker stoneware. Drain all but 1 tbsp (15 mL) oil from pan.

4. Reduce heat to medium. Add onions, carrots and celery to pan and cook, stirring, until softened. Add garlic, rosemary and orange zest and cook, stirring, for 1 minute. Sprinkle reserved flour mixture over vegetables and cook, stirring, for 1 minute. Add orange juice, beef broth and wine and bring to a boil.

5. Pour mixture over lamb, cover and cook on **Low** for 12 hours or on **High** for 6 hours, until lamb is falling off the bone. Transfer lamb and beans to a deep platter or serving dish and keep warm. In a saucepan over medium-high heat, reduce cooking liquid by one-third. Pour over lamb and garnish liberally with parsley.

TIPS
• Legumes are usually cooked before being added to a casserole, but with an overnight soak, they cook beautifully in this aromatic broth.
• If you prefer more assertive flavors, bury a whole branch of fresh rosemary, stem and all, in the lamb before adding the sauce.

Poultry

Chicken with 40 Cloves of Garlic

Chicken with 40 Cloves of Garlic

SERVES 6

My favorite version of this classic French dish was popularized by the late James Beard, the great guru of American cooking. When I was just beginning my career as a food writer, I had the pleasure of spending a week in New York, cooking with him at his West Village townhouse. He was a charming and generous man, and many of the lessons he taught me then have served me well throughout the years. This is great bistro fare and my favorite kind of food — simple and flavorful. Serve with lots of mashed potatoes or toasted slices of baguette to soak up the sauce.

MAKE AHEAD
This dish can be partially prepared the night before it is cooked. Complete Steps 1 and 3. Cover and refrigerate overnight. The next morning, brown chicken (Step 2), or if you're pressed for time, continue cooking as directed.

2 tbsp	butter	25 mL
40	cloves garlic, peeled (about 4 heads)	40
3½ lbs	chicken pieces, skin on breasts, skinless legs and thighs	1.75 kg
2	onions, finely chopped	2
4	stalks celery, peeled and diced	4
1 tsp	dried tarragon leaves (see Tips, below)	5 mL
1 tsp	salt	5 mL
½ tsp	cracked black peppercorns	2 mL
¼ tsp	freshly grated nutmeg	1 mL
½ cup	dry white vermouth or white wine	125 mL

1. In a skillet, melt butter over medium-low heat. Add garlic and cook, stirring often, until it softens and begins to turn golden. With a slotted spoon, transfer to slow cooker stoneware.

2. Increase heat to medium. Add chicken, in batches, and brown. Transfer to slow cooker stoneware.

3. Add onions and celery to pan and cook, stirring, until softened. Add tarragon, salt, peppercorns and nutmeg and cook, stirring, for 1 minute. Add vermouth and bring to a boil.

4. Pour over chicken. Cover and cook on **Low** for 5 to 6 hours or on **High** for 2½ to 3 hours, until juices run clear when pierced with a fork.

TIPS
• If you don't like the taste of tarragon, substitute 1 tsp (5 mL) dried thyme leaves.
• Softening the garlic in butter before adding it to the sauce helps to mellow its strong flavor.

Chicken and Barley

SERVES 6

I love the simple but appetizing combination of flavors in this delicious dish. Although we usually eat this as a family dinner, all it takes is a dressed-up salad — try a combination of Boston lettuce, mesclun greens, red onion and avocado in a balsamic vinaigrette — crusty rolls and some crisp white wine to make it perfect for guests.

MAKE AHEAD
This dish can be partially prepared the night before it is cooked. Complete Step 2, heating 1 tbsp (15 mL) oil in pan before softening vegetables. Cover and refrigerate overnight. The next morning, brown chicken (Step 1), or if you're pressed for time, omit this step and place chicken directly in slow cooker stoneware and continue cooking as directed in Step 3.

1 tbsp	vegetable oil	15 mL
3 lbs	chicken pieces, skin on breasts, skinless legs and thighs	1.5 kg
2	onions, chopped	2
4	stalks celery, peeled and diced	4
4	cloves garlic, minced	4
1 tsp	salt	5 mL
½ tsp	cracked black peppercorns	2 mL
½ tsp	dried thyme leaves	2 mL
1 cup	pearl barley, rinsed	250 mL
1	can (28 oz/796 mL) tomatoes, including juice, coarsely chopped	1
1 cup	dry white wine or chicken stock	250 mL
2	red bell peppers, chopped	2
	Finely chopped dill	

1. In a skillet, heat oil over medium-high heat. Add chicken, in batches, and brown. Transfer to slow cooker stoneware.

2. Reduce heat to medium. Add onions and celery to pan and cook, stirring, until softened. Add garlic, salt, peppercorns and thyme and cook, stirring, for 1 minute. Add barley and stir until coated. Add tomatoes and wine and bring to a boil.

3. Pour mixture over chicken. Cover and cook on **Low** for 6 hours or on **High** for 3 hours, until juices run clear when chicken is pierced with a fork. Add peppers and cook on **High** for 15 minutes, until softened. Transfer mixture to a deep platter and garnish liberally with dill. Serve piping hot.

Spanish-Style Chicken with Rice

SERVES 6

....

Here's a slow cooker version of the great Spanish dish Arroz con Pollo. *This tasty one-dish meal is popular with everyone, especially my husband, who always has seconds. Serve with a green salad and hot crusty bread, and pass the hot pepper sauce for those who like heat.*

¼ tsp	saffron threads, soaked in 2 tbsp (25 mL) boiling water, or 1 tsp (5 mL) turmeric (see Pantry Notes, page 141)	1 mL
1 tbsp	vegetable oil	15 mL
3 lbs	chicken pieces, skin on breasts, skinless legs and thighs	1.5 kg
2	onions, finely chopped	2
4	cloves garlic, minced	4
1 tsp	salt	5 mL
¼ tsp	freshly ground black pepper	1 mL
1½ cups	long-grain converted rice	375 mL
1	can (28 oz/796 mL) tomatoes, including juice, chopped	1
1½ cups	chicken stock or 1 cup (250 mL) chicken stock plus ½ cup (125 mL) dry white wine	375 mL
1	green bell pepper, finely chopped	1
1 cup	green peas, thawed if frozen	250 mL
	Sliced pimento-stuffed green olives, optional	
	Hot pepper sauce, optional	

1. In a nonstick skillet, heat oil over medium-high heat. Add chicken, in batches, and brown lightly on all sides. Transfer to slow cooker stoneware.

2. Reduce heat to medium. Add onions and cook, stirring, until softened. Add garlic, salt and pepper and cook, stirring, for 1 minute. Add rice and stir until grains are well coated with mixture. Stir in saffron, tomatoes and chicken stock. Transfer to slow cooker stoneware and stir to combine with chicken.

3. Cover and cook on **Low** for 6 to 8 hours or on **High** for 3 to 4 hours, until juices run clear when chicken is pierced with a fork. Stir in green pepper and peas, cover and cook on **High** for 20 minutes, until vegetables are heated through. Garnish with olives, if using, and pass hot pepper sauce, if using.

....

TIP

• If you are in a hurry, skip browning the chicken. Just make sure that all the skin is removed; otherwise the dish will be too fatty.

The Captain's Curry

This style of curry, made with a creamed curry sauce, was popular in the great American seaports during the 19th century. It gets its name from sea captains involved in the spice trade, who brought their wares to cities such as Charleston. Traditionally, the chicken is cooked separately, and the meat is shredded or cut into small pieces. Then the reserved broth is used to make the curry sauce. Today, we associate coconut milk with our current interest in Asian foods. But citizens of the old South were quite familiar with this ingredient, which they made themselves using fresh coconuts from the West Indies.

MAKE AHEAD
Complete Step 2, heating 1 tbsp (15 mL) oil in pan before softening onions. Cover and refrigerate overnight. The next morning, brown chicken (Step 1), or omit this step and continue cooking as directed in Step 3.

1 tbsp	vegetable oil	15 mL
3 lbs	chicken pieces, skin on breasts, skinless legs and thighs	1.5 kg
2	onions, finely chopped	2
2	stalks celery, peeled and thinly sliced	2
2	cloves garlic, minced	2
1 tbsp	curry powder	15 mL
½ tsp	chili powder	2 mL
½ tsp	ground allspice	2 mL
½ tsp	freshly grated nutmeg	2 mL
1	cinnamon stick piece, about 3 inches (7.5 cm) long	1
1	bay leaf	1
2 tbsp	all-purpose flour	25 mL
1	can (10 oz/284 mL) condensed chicken broth, undiluted	1
2	apples, peeled and diced	2
1 cup	coconut milk	250 mL
	Toasted sliced almonds, optional	
	Hot white rice	
	Mango chutney, optional	

1. In a nonstick skillet, heat oil over medium-high heat. Add chicken, in batches, and brown on all sides. Transfer to slow cooker stoneware.

2. Reduce heat to medium. Add onions and celery and cook, stirring, until softened. Add garlic, curry powder, chili powder, allspice, nutmeg, cinnamon stick and bay leaf and cook, stirring, for 1 minute. Sprinkle flour over mixture and cook, stirring, for 1 minute. Add chicken broth, bring to a boil and cook, stirring, until thickened. Stir in apples.

3. Pour mixture over chicken, cover and cook on **Low** for 5 to 6 hours or on **High** for 2½ to 3 hours, until juices run clear when chicken is pierced with a fork. Stir in coconut milk and cook until heated through. Discard cinnamon stick and bay leaf. Garnish with almonds, if using, and serve over hot white rice, accompanied by chutney, if desired.

Chicken in Onion Buttermilk Gravy

SERVES 4 TO 6

Here's a dish that is reminiscent of the old South — a rich onion-flavored gravy, punctuated with peas and finished with buttermilk to add a hint of tartness. I like to serve this with mounds of steamy mashed potatoes, sprinkled with finely chopped parsley, to soak up the sauce. Serve leftovers over hot buttermilk biscuits for a truly delicious lunch.

MAKE AHEAD
This dish can be partially prepared the night before it is cooked. Complete Step 2, heating 1 tbsp (15 mL) oil in pan before softening onions. Cover and refrigerate overnight. The next morning, brown chicken (Step 1), or if you're pressed for time, omit this step and place chicken directly in slow cooker stoneware. Continue cooking as directed in Step 3.

1 tbsp	vegetable oil	15 mL
3 lbs	chicken pieces, skin on breasts, skinless legs and thighs	1.5 kg
6	onions, sliced paper-thin	6
1 tsp	salt	5 mL
1/2 tsp	cracked black peppercorns	2 mL
1/2 tsp	dried thyme leaves	2 mL
1/4 cup	all-purpose flour	50 mL
1	can (10 oz/284 mL) condensed chicken broth, undiluted	1
1	bay leaf	1
1 1/2 cups	green peas, thawed if frozen	375 mL
3/4 cup	buttermilk (see Tip, below)	175 mL

1. In a nonstick skillet, heat oil over medium-high heat. Add chicken, in batches, and brown lightly on all sides. Transfer to slow cooker stoneware.

2. Reduce heat to medium. Add onions to pan and cook, stirring, until softened and just beginning to turn brown. Add salt, peppercorns and thyme and cook, stirring, for 1 minute. Sprinkle flour over mixture, stir well and cook for 1 minute. Add chicken broth and bay leaf and cook, stirring, until mixture thickens.

3. Pour mixture over chicken. Cover and cook on **Low** for 6 hours or on **High** for 3 hours, until juices run clear when chicken is pierced with a fork. Stir in peas and buttermilk. Cover and cook on **High** for 20 minutes, until peas are cooked. Discard bay leaf.

TIP
• If you don't have buttermilk, use 1/2 cup (125 mL) milk mixed with 3 tbsp (45 mL) sour cream.

Chicken 'n' Dumplings

SERVES 4 TO 6

There is something quintessentially comforting about chicken and dumplings. Perhaps it is the familiar flavors in the simple chicken stew or the gentle blandness of the dumplings, which suggests a willingness to accommodate whatever comes their way. In any case, this is delicious family-style fare.

MAKE AHEAD
This dish can be partially prepared the night before it is cooked. Complete Step 2, heating 1 tbsp (15 mL) oil in pan before softening vegetables. Cover and refrigerate overnight. The next morning, brown chicken (Step 1), or if you're pressed for time, omit this step and place chicken directly in slow cooker stoneware. Continue cooking as directed in Step 3.

1 tbsp	vegetable oil	15 mL
3 lbs	chicken pieces, skin on breasts, skinless legs and thighs	1.5 kg
2	medium onions, finely chopped	2
4	carrots, peeled and thinly sliced	4
4	stalks celery, peeled and thinly sliced	4
1 tsp	dried tarragon or thyme leaves	5 mL
1 tsp	salt	5 mL
1/2 tsp	cracked black peppercorns	2 mL
1/4 cup	all-purpose flour	50 mL
1 cup	condensed chicken broth, undiluted	250 mL
1/2 cup	dry white wine or condensed chicken broth	125 mL
1 cup	green peas, thawed if frozen	250 mL
1/2 cup	whipping cream, optional	125 mL

Dumplings

1 1/4 cups	sifted all-purpose flour	300 mL
2 tsp	baking powder	10 mL
1/2 tsp	salt	2 mL
1/4 cup	finely chopped fresh parsley, optional	50 mL
2 tbsp	melted butter	25 mL
3/4 cup	warm milk	175 mL

1. In a nonstick skillet, heat oil over medium-high heat. Add chicken, in batches, and brown lightly on all sides. Transfer to slow cooker stoneware.

2. Reduce heat to medium. Add onions, carrots and celery to pan and cook, stirring, until vegetables are softened. Add tarragon, salt and peppercorns and cook, stirring, for 1 minute. Sprinkle flour over mixture, stir well and cook for 1 minute. Add chicken broth and wine and cook, stirring, until thickened.

3. Pour mixture over chicken. Cover and cook on **Low** for 5 to 6 hours or on **High** for 3 hours, until juices run clear when chicken is pierced with a fork. Stir in peas and whipping cream, if using.

continued on page 138

4. Dumplings: Turn slow cooker heat to **High**. In a bowl, combine flour, baking powder, salt and parsley, if using. Add butter and milk and stir just until moistened (lumps are fine). Drop dumpling dough, by spoonfuls, onto hot chicken. Cover and cook on **High** for 30 minutes or until a toothpick inserted in center of dumplings comes out clean.

TIP

• There are several steps you can take to ensure that your dumplings are as light and fluffy as possible. Preheat the slow cooker to **High** so the stew will be bubbling when you add the dumplings. Sift the flour before measuring and warm the milk before adding to the dry ingredients. Drop the batter directly onto pieces of chicken. If the batter is submerged in the liquid, the dumplings will be soggy.

PANTRY NOTES

Cracked Black Peppercorns
I recommend the use of cracked black peppercorns rather than ground pepper in many of my recipes because they release flavor slowly during the long cooking process. "Cracked pepper" can be purchased in the spice sections of supermarkets, but I like to make my own in a mortar with a pestle. A rolling pin or even a heavy can on its side will also break up the peppercorns for use in slow cooked dishes. If you prefer to use ground black pepper, use one-quarter to one-half the amount of cracked black peppercorns called for in the recipe.

Curried Chicken with Spinach

SERVES 6

This tasty curry is delicious over hot cooked rice. If you want to extend the quantity, try the variation with lentils.

MAKE AHEAD
This dish can be partially prepared the night before it is cooked. Complete Step 1. Cover and refrigerate overnight. The next morning, continue with Step 2.

1 tbsp	vegetable oil	15 mL
2	onions, finely chopped	2
2	cloves garlic, minced	2
1 tsp	minced gingerroot	5 mL
1	long red or green chili pepper, finely chopped	1
1 tbsp	each turmeric and cumin seeds	15 mL
1 tsp	salt	5 mL
1/2 tsp	cracked black peppercorns	2 mL
1/2 tsp	ground coriander seeds	2 mL
1	cinnamon stick piece, about 2 inches (5 cm)	1
1	can (28 oz/796 mL) tomatoes, drained and chopped	1
1/2 cup	condensed chicken broth, undiluted	125 mL
1	bay leaf	1
3 1/2 lbs	chicken pieces, skin on breasts, skinless legs and thighs	1.75 kg
1 lb	fresh spinach leaves or 1 package (10 oz/300 g) spinach, washed, stems removed and coarsely chopped	500 g
1/2 cup	plain yogurt	125 mL
	Hot cooked rice	

1. In a skillet, heat oil over medium heat. Add onion and cook, stirring, until it begins to brown. Add garlic, gingerroot, chili pepper, turmeric, cumin seeds, peppercorns, coriander and cinnamon stick and cook, stirring, for 1 minute. Add tomatoes, chicken broth and bay leaf and bring to a boil. Remove from heat.

2. Place chicken in slow cooker stoneware and cover with sauce. Cover and cook on **Low** for 5 to 6 hours or on **High** for 2 1/2 to 3 hours, until juices run clear when pierced with a fork. Stir in spinach and yogurt. Cover and cook on **High** for 20 minutes, until spinach is cooked. Serve over rice.

VARIATION
Curried Chicken with Spinach and Lentils: In a saucepan, bring 3 cups (750 mL) water to a boil. Add 1/2 cup (125 mL) brown lentils. Cover and return water to a boil. Turn off heat and allow to rest. Proceed with the recipe. Add drained lentils to stoneware along with the chicken and continue cooking as directed, but omit the yogurt.

Chicken and Chickpeas with Spinach

SERVES 4 TO 6

....

Delicious and nutritious, with tantalizing Middle Eastern flavors of lemon and cumin, this is a great one-dish meal. To dress it up and continue the Middle Eastern theme, serve with a salad of roasted red peppers tossed in extra-virgin olive oil and hot pita bread.

MAKE AHEAD
This dish can be partially prepared the night before it is cooked. Complete Step 2, heating 1 tbsp (15 mL) oil in pan before softening onions. Cover and refrigerate overnight. The next morning, brown chicken (Step 1), or if you're pressed for time, omit browning and place chicken directly in slow cooker stoneware. Continue cooking as directed in Step 3.

¼ tsp	saffron threads, soaked in 2 tbsp (25 mL) boiling water, or 1 tsp (5 mL) turmeric	1 mL
1 tbsp	vegetable oil	15 mL
3½ lbs	chicken pieces, skin on breasts, skinless legs and thighs	1.75 kg
2	onions, finely chopped	2
4	cloves garlic, minced	4
1	long red or green chili pepper, finely chopped, optional	1
2 tbsp	cumin seeds	25 mL
1 tsp	salt	5 mL
½ tsp	cracked black peppercorns	2 mL
1	can (10 oz/284 mL) condensed chicken broth, undiluted	1
1 tsp	grated lemon zest	5 mL
2 tbsp	freshly squeezed lemon juice	25 mL
1	can (19 oz/540 mL) chickpeas, drained and rinsed, or 1 cup (250 mL) dried chickpeas, soaked, cooked and drained	1
1 lb	fresh spinach leaves or 1 package (10 oz/300 g) spinach, washed, stems removed and chopped (see Tip, right)	500 g

1. In a nonstick skillet, heat oil over medium-high heat. Add chicken, in batches, and brown on all sides. Transfer to slow cooker stoneware.

2. Reduce heat to medium. Add onions to pan and cook, stirring, until softened. Add garlic, chili pepper, if using, cumin seeds, saffron, salt and peppercorns and cook, stirring, for 1 minute. Add chicken broth, lemon zest, lemon juice and chickpeas and bring to a boil.

3. Pour mixture over chicken, cover and cook on **Low** for 5 to 6 hours or on **High** for 2½ to 3 hours, until juices run clear when chicken is pierced with a fork. Add spinach, stirring to combine as best you can. Cover and cook on **High** for 20 minutes, until spinach is cooked.

TIP

• If you are using spinach leaves in this recipe, take care to wash them thoroughly, as they can be quite gritty. To wash spinach, fill a clean sink with lukewarm water. Remove the tough stems and submerge the tender leaves in the water, swishing to remove the grit. Rinse thoroughly in a colander under cold running water, checking carefully to ensure that no sand remains.

PANTRY NOTES

Saffron
Saffron is a pungent, bittersweet spice garnered from a particular kind of crocus. It is difficult to harvest and, therefore, expensive. However, a little goes a long way. Buy saffron in threads, not powder, preferably from a reputable purveyor. Turmeric can be used to convey the saffron color in a dish, but it will not replicate the unique and haunting flavor of the original.

Chilies
Long red or green chilies, which are narrow and about 3 inches (7.5 cm) in length, with a sharply pointed end, are probably the most versatile member of the chili family. Fairly hot, they are commonly used in Indian and Szechuan cooking and can be substituted for most other chilies. If you can't find them in your supermarket, look for them in Asian groceries. Sometimes they are identified as serrano chilies.

African-Style Braised Chicken in Peanut Sauce

SERVES 6

The combination of chicken with a spicy peanut sauce is usually associated with Thai food, where grilled chicken satay is served as an appetizer with peanut sauce on the side. Here's an unusual and delicious recipe that moves the delectable combination of hot peppers and peanuts into the main course. Serve with plenty of hot white rice.

MAKE AHEAD
This dish can be partially prepared the night before it is cooked. Complete Step 2, heating 1 tbsp (15 mL) oil in pan before softening onions. Cover and refrigerate overnight. The next morning, brown chicken (Step 1), or if you're pressed for time, omit this step and place chicken directly in slow cooker stoneware. Continue cooking as directed in Step 3.

1 tbsp	vegetable oil	15 mL
3 lbs	chicken pieces, skin on breasts, skinless legs and thighs	1.5 kg
2	onions, finely chopped	2
4	cloves garlic, minced	4
½ to 1	long red or green chili pepper, minced	½ to 1
2 tsp	curry powder	10 mL
1 tsp	dried oregano leaves	5 mL
1 tsp	salt	5 mL
½ tsp	cracked black peppercorns	2 mL
½ cup	condensed chicken broth, undiluted	125 mL
½ cup	tomato sauce	125 mL
1	bay leaf	1
½ cup	peanut butter	125 mL
2 tbsp	sherry or lemon juice	25 mL
1	red bell pepper, finely chopped	1
	Hot white rice	

1. In a nonstick skillet, heat oil over medium-high heat. Add chicken, in batches, and brown on all sides. Transfer to slow cooker stoneware.

2. Reduce heat to medium. Add onions and cook, stirring, until softened. Add garlic, chili pepper, curry powder, oregano, salt and peppercorns and cook, stirring, for 1 minute. Stir in chicken broth, tomato sauce and bay leaf and bring to a boil.

3. Pour mixture over chicken. Cover and cook on **Low** for 6 hours or on **High** for 3 hours, until juices run clear when chicken is pierced with a fork.

4. In a bowl, combine peanut butter and sherry. Add a little cooking liquid and stir to blend. Add to slow cooker along with red pepper. Cover and cook on **High** for 20 minutes, until pepper is tender. Discard bay leaf. Serve over hot white rice.

Chicken Enchiladas in Tomatillo Sauce

SERVES 6

This creamy and flavorful casserole is my idea of Mexican comfort food. Fully garnished, with avocados, tomatoes and lettuce, it is a meal in itself.

MAKE AHEAD
This dish can be partially prepared the night before it is cooked. Complete Steps 1 and 2. Cover and refrigerate sauce overnight. The next morning, continue cooking as directed, spooning the sauce over the filled tortillas as it will have thickened overnight.

• *Large (minimum 5 quart) oval slow cooker*

1	dried ancho chili pepper	1
1 cup	boiling water	250 mL
4 cups	shredded and cooked chicken, about 3 lbs (1.5 kg) bone-in chicken (see Tips, right)	1 L
1 tbsp	vegetable oil	15 mL
2	onions, finely chopped	2
4	cloves garlic, minced	4
1 to 2	jalapeño peppers, finely chopped	1 to 2
1 tbsp	dried oregano leaves	15 mL
1	can (28 oz/796 mL) tomatillos, drained and chopped (see Tips, right)	1
4 oz	cream cheese, cut into cubes	125 g
½ cup	chicken stock	125 mL
1 tbsp	lime juice	15 mL
12	medium tortillas (corn or flour)	12
½ cup	finely chopped green onion	125 mL
¼ cup	finely chopped cilantro	50 mL
2 cups	shredded Monterey Jack cheese	500 mL
	Finely chopped cilantro, optional	
	Shredded lettuce, optional	
	Chopped tomato, optional	
	Sliced avocado, optional	

1. In a heatproof bowl, soak dried chili in boiling water for 30 minutes, making sure that all parts of the pepper are submerged. Drain and discard water. Coarsely chop and set aside.

2. In a skillet, heat oil over medium heat. Add onion and cook, stirring, until softened. Add garlic, jalapeño pepper, oregano and reserved chili pepper and cook, stirring, for 1 minute. Add tomatillos and cream cheese and cook, stirring, until cheese melts. Remove from heat.

3. In a bowl, combine chicken stock and lime juice. One at a time, dip tortillas in mixture, turning to ensure all parts are moistened. Lay a tortilla on a plate and spread with about $\frac{1}{3}$ cup (75 mL) shredded chicken. Sprinkle with approximately 1 tsp (5 mL) each green onion and cilantro and 2 tbsp (25 mL) shredded cheese. (You will have about $\frac{1}{2}$ cup/125 mL cheese left over.) Fold ends over and roll up. Discard remaining broth mixture.

4. Lay filled tortillas, seam side down, in slow cooker stoneware. Pour sauce over tortillas and sprinkle with remaining cheese.

5. Cover and cook on **Low** for 7 to 8 hours or on **High** for 3 to 4 hours, until hot and bubbling. Garnish with any combination of cilantro, shredded lettuce, chopped tomato and sliced avocado.

TIPS

• You can use leftover chicken in this recipe or you can easily make shredded chicken by cooking the chicken in the broth when making Mexican Chicken Soup (see recipe, page 56). Add the required amount of chicken to the broth, then separate it from the quantity required for the soup after it has cooked. Shred and refrigerate until ready to use.

• Tomatillos are a small, green tomato-like fruit with a unique citrus taste. They are available in many supermarkets and specialty food stores selling Latin American products.

Cheesy Jalapeño Chicken Loaf

SERVES 6 TO 8

....

Here's a chicken loaf that is tasty and flavorful. Add the cream cheese if you prefer a creamier texture and are not concerned about fat.

2 lbs	ground chicken	1 kg
½ cup	fresh bread crumbs	125 mL
2	onions, finely chopped	2
2	cloves garlic, minced	2
1 to 2	jalapeño peppers, finely chopped	1 to 2
1 tsp	ground cumin	5 mL
2 tsp	dried oregano leaves	10 mL
1 tsp	salt	5 mL
¼ tsp	freshly ground black pepper	1 mL
2 tbsp	Worcestershire sauce	25 mL
2	eggs, beaten	2
1 cup	shredded Monterey Jack cheese	250 mL
4 oz	cream cheese, cut into ¼-inch (0.5 cm) cubes, optional	125 g

1. Fold a 2-foot (60 cm) piece of foil in half lengthwise. Place on bottom and up sides of slow cooker stoneware.

2. In a large bowl, combine all the ingredients, including cream cheese, if using, and mix well. Shape into a loaf and place on foil in slow cooker stoneware. Cover and cook on **Low** for 8 to 10 hours or on **High** for 4 to 5 hours, or until juices run clear when loaf is pierced with a fork or meat thermometer reads 170°F (80°C).

....

VARIATION
Cheesy Jalapeño Turkey Loaf: Substitute 2 lbs (1 kg) ground turkey for the chicken.

Spicy Chicken Stew with Cornmeal Dumplings

SERVES 6

····································

This lively and unusual chicken stew has just a hint of the old Southwest. Although any kind of fresh chili pepper works well in this recipe, using one jalapeño pepper and one chipotle pepper in adobo sauce will establish the Southwestern flavors more firmly.

MAKE AHEAD
This dish can be partially prepared the night before it is cooked. Complete Step 2, heating 1 tbsp (15 mL) oil in pan before softening onions. Cover and refrigerate overnight. The next morning, brown chicken (Step 1), or if you're pressed for time, omit this step and place chicken directly in slow cooker stoneware. Continue cooking as directed in Step 3.

1 tbsp	vegetable oil	15 mL
3½ lbs	chicken pieces, skin on breasts, skinless legs and thighs	1.75 kg
2	onions, finely chopped	2
4	stalks celery, peeled and diced	4
4	cloves garlic, minced	4
1 to 2	fresh chili peppers, seeded and finely chopped (see left)	1 to 2
2 tsp	dried oregano leaves	10 mL
1 tsp	cumin seeds	5 mL
1 tsp	salt	5 mL
½ tsp	cracked black peppercorns	2 mL
1 tbsp	coarse mustard	15 mL
¼ cup	tomato paste	50 mL
2 tbsp	all-purpose flour	25 mL
½ cup	dry white wine or water	125 mL
½ cup	condensed chicken broth (undiluted)	125 mL

Cornmeal Dumplings

¾ cup	sifted all-purpose flour	175 mL
¼ cup	fine cornmeal	50 mL
1½ tsp	baking powder	7 mL
¼ tsp	salt	1 mL
½ cup	warm milk	125 mL
2 tbsp	melted butter	25 mL

1. In a skillet, heat oil over medium-high heat. Add chicken, in batches, and brown on all sides. Transfer to slow cooker stoneware. Reduce heat to medium.

2. Add onions and celery to pan and cook, stirring, until softened. Add garlic, chili pepper, oregano, cumin seeds, salt and peppercorns and cook, stirring, for 1 minute. Stir in mustard and tomato paste. Sprinkle flour over mixture and cook, stirring, for 1 minute. Add wine and chicken broth and cook, stirring, until thickened.

3. Pour over chicken, cover and cook on **Low** for 5 to 6 hours or on **High** for $2\frac{1}{2}$ to 3 hours, until juices run clear when pierced with a fork.

4. Cornmeal Dumplings: Turn slow cooker heat to **High**. In a bowl, combine flour, cornmeal, baking powder and salt. Make a well in the center. Pour in milk and butter and mix with a fork, just until the mixture comes together. Drop dough by spoonfuls onto chicken pieces. Cover and cook on **High** for 30 minutes, until a tester inserted in the center comes out clean.

TIP
- Sifting the flour before measuring it helps to ensure that dumplings will have a lighter texture, as does warming the milk and turning the slow cooker heat to **High** before you start to mix.

PANTRY NOTES

Chipotle Peppers
Chipotle peppers are usually available canned in adobo sauce. Since there are few dishes that require more than one or two of these robust little devils (I find that their smoky taste, even more than their heat, goes a long way), it is helpful that they freeze well. I separate the peppers left over from a can into batches of two and freeze them, with sauce, in small freezer bags. That way, I always have a supply on hand.

Balsamic Braised Chicken with Olives

SERVES 6

·····································

Here's a tasty Mediterranean-inspired dish that is simple yet elegant. Serve this over creamy Slow-Cooked Polenta (see recipe, page 211) or hot couscous for a delectable meal.

MAKE AHEAD
This dish can be partially prepared the night before it is cooked. Complete Step 2, heating 1 tbsp (15 mL) oil in pan before softening onions. The next day, brown chicken (Step 1), or if you're pressed for time, omit this step and add chicken directly to slow cooker stoneware. Continue cooking as directed in Step 3.

1 tbsp	vegetable oil	15 mL
3½ lbs	chicken pieces, skin on breasts, skinless legs and thighs	1.75 kg
2	onions, finely chopped	2
4	cloves garlic, minced	4
1 tsp	salt	5 mL
½ tsp	cracked black peppercorns	2 mL
½ tsp	dried thyme leaves	2 mL
2 cups	chopped peeled tomatoes, including juice, if canned	500 mL
½ cup	condensed chicken broth, undiluted	125 mL
2 tbsp	balsamic vinegar	25 mL
2 tbsp	chopped black olives	25 mL
2 tbsp	capers, optional	25 mL

1. In a nonstick skillet, heat oil over medium-high heat. Add chicken, in batches, and brown. Transfer to slow cooker stoneware. Reduce heat to medium.

2. Add onions to pan and cook, stirring, until softened. Add garlic, salt, peppercorns and thyme and cook, stirring, for 1 minute. Add tomatoes, chicken broth and balsamic vinegar and bring to a boil.

3. Pour mixture over chicken. Cover and cook on **Low** for 5 to 6 hours or on **High** for 2½ to 3 hours, until juices run clear when chicken is pierced with a fork. Add olives and capers, if using, and stir well. Serve immediately.

Pulled Turkey

SERVES 6 TO 8

....

Here's a lower-fat variation on the theme of pulled pork, a barbecue favorite from the South. If you like a more intensely smoky flavor, increase the quantity of liquid smoke, but be careful — a little goes a long way. Serve this between hot split onion or Kaiser buns, accompanied by a bowl of coleslaw for a "down-home" dinner that all will enjoy.

MAKE AHEAD
This dish can be partially prepared the night before it is cooked. Complete Step 2. Cover and refrigerate sauce overnight. The next morning, continue as directed in Steps 1, 3 and 4.

3 to 4 lbs	turkey legs or breast, skin removed	1.5 to 2 kg
1	small onion, grated	1
2	cloves garlic, minced	2
1/2 cup	tomato ketchup	125 mL
1/3 cup	corn syrup	75 mL
1/4 cup	Dijon or coarse mustard	50 mL
2 tbsp	cider vinegar	25 mL
1 tbsp	chili powder	15 mL
1/2 tsp	salt	2 mL
1/2 tsp	cracked black peppercorns	2 mL
1 tbsp	Worcestershire sauce	15 mL
1/2 tsp	liquid smoke	2 mL
	Warm buns	

1. Place turkey in slow cooker stoneware.

2. In a saucepan over medium heat, combine remaining ingredients except for liquid smoke. Bring to boil and simmer for 5 minutes. Remove from heat and stir in liquid smoke.

3. Pour sauce over turkey. Cover and cook on **Low** for 8 to 10 hours or on **High** for 4 to 5 hours, until turkey is falling apart.

4. Transfer turkey to a cutting board and pull meat off the bones in shreds, using two forks. Return to sauce and keep warm. When ready to serve, spoon shredded turkey and sauce over warm buns.

Turkey Sloppy Joes

SERVES 6

....

Kids love this savory mixture, which is perfect for those busy evenings when you have to rush out after eating dinner. Serve this over hot split onion buns and accompany with a tossed salad for a tasty and nutritious meal.

MAKE AHEAD
This dish can be partially prepared the night before it is cooked. Complete Steps 1 and 2, chilling cooked meat and onion mixtures separately. Cover and refrigerate. The next morning, combine and continue cooking as directed in Step 3.

2 tbsp	vegetable oil, divided	25 mL
1 ½ lbs	ground turkey	750 g
2	onions, finely chopped	2
4	cloves garlic, minced	4
1	jalapeño pepper, minced, optional	1
1 tbsp	chili powder	15 mL
2 tsp	dried oregano leaves	10 mL
1 tsp	salt	5 mL
¼ tsp	freshly ground black pepper	1 mL
1 cup	tomato-based chili sauce	250 mL
1 tbsp	Worcestershire sauce	15 mL
2 cups	shredded Monterey Jack cheese	500 mL
1	green bell pepper, finely chopped, optional	1
	Hot onion buns	

1. In a skillet, heat 1 tbsp (15 mL) oil over medium heat. Add turkey and cook, breaking up meat with a wooden spoon, until no longer pink. Using a slotted spoon, transfer to slow cooker stoneware. Drain and discard liquid.

2. Add remaining oil to pan. Add onions and cook, stirring, until softened. Add garlic, jalapeño pepper, if using, chili powder, oregano, salt and black pepper and cook, stirring, for 1 minute. Add chili sauce and Worcestershire sauce and bring to a boil.

3. Transfer mixture to slow cooker stoneware. Cover and cook on **Low** for 8 to 10 hours or on **High** for 4 to 5 hours, until mixture is hot and bubbling. Add cheese and green pepper, if using. Cover and cook on **High** for 20 minutes, until cheese is melted and pepper is softened. Spoon over hot split onion buns and serve.

Turkey and Sausage Chili

SERVES 8

I love the slightly smoky flavor of the New Mexico chilies in this delicious chili. Use hot or mild Italian sausage depending upon your preference, and if you are very fond of heat, add an extra jalapeño pepper or, better still, a chopped chipotle pepper in adobo sauce, which will intensify the smoky flavor, as well as adding heat.

MAKE AHEAD
This dish can be partially prepared the night before it is cooked. Complete Steps 1, 2, 3 and 5, draining off fat in pan before softening onions. Combine cooked sausage with vegetable mixture, cover and refrigerate overnight. The next morning, brown turkey (Step 4), or if you're pressed for time, omit this step and place directly in slow cooker stoneware. Continue with Step 6.

2	dried New Mexico chili peppers	2
2 cups	boiling water	500 mL
1 tbsp	cumin seeds	15 mL
1 tbsp	vegetable oil	15 mL
1 lb	Italian or soft chorizo sausage, removed from casings	500 g
2 lbs	skinless boneless turkey breast or thighs, cut into 1-inch (2.5 cm) cubes	1 kg
2	onions, finely chopped	2
6	cloves garlic, minced	6
1	jalapeño pepper, finely chopped, optional	1
1 tbsp	dried oregano leaves	15 mL
1 tsp	salt	5 mL
1 tsp	cracked black peppercorns	5 mL
1	can (28 oz/796 mL) tomatoes, including juice	1
2 cups	flat beer or chicken stock	500 mL
2	cans (19 oz/540 mL) kidney or pinto beans, drained and rinsed, or 2 cups (500 mL) dried kidney or pinto beans, cooked and drained (see Basic Beans, page 214)	2
	Sour cream, optional	
	Salsa, optional	
	Shredded Monterey Jack cheese, optional	
	Crushed tortilla chips, optional	

1. In a heatproof bowl, soak chilies in boiling water for 30 minutes. Drain and discard stems and liquid. Pat dry with paper towel and set aside.

2. In a skillet, toast cumin seeds over medium heat, stirring constantly, until they release their aroma and begin to turn brown. Immediately transfer to a small bowl and set aside.

3. In the same skillet, heat oil over medium-high heat. Add sausage and cook, stirring, until no longer pink. Transfer to slow cooker stoneware with a slotted spoon.

4. Add turkey to pan, in batches, and brown. Transfer to slow cooker stoneware. Drain all but 1 tbsp (15 mL) fat from pan. Reduce heat to medium.

5. Add onions to pan and cook, stirring, until softened. Add garlic, jalapeño pepper, if using, oregano, salt, peppercorns, reserved cumin seeds and chili peppers and cook, stirring, for 1 minute. Transfer contents of pan to food processor. Add tomatoes and process until smooth.

6. Pour mixture over meat. Add beer and beans to slow cooker stoneware and stir to combine. Cover and cook on **Low** for 8 to 10 hours or on **High** for 4 to 5 hours, until turkey is no longer pink inside.

7. To serve, ladle into soup bowls and garnish with any combination of sour cream, salsa, Monterey Jack cheese and crushed tortilla chips.

PANTRY NOTES

New Mexico Chili Peppers
These long pointed chilies are larger and milder than most and have a slightly smoky flavor that imparts a Southwestern tang to soups and stews. Like many more "exotic" chilies, they are now available in dried form in the produce section of many supermarkets. If the dried chilies are not thoroughly rehydrated for 30 minutes in boiling water, I've found that they impart a bitter flavor to recipes. If you can't find New Mexico chilies, I recommend adding a mild smoky hot pepper sauce, to taste, after the dish is cooked.

Turkey in Puff Pastry

SERVES 6 TO 8

I've always enjoyed the many variations of this comfort food classic. Here, succulent chunks of turkey are served in a creamy sauce embellished with mushrooms and sweet red pepper. The velvety sauce contrasts with the crunchy crust of a vol-au-vent. For a celebratory dinner, add a salad of mushrooms, bacon bits and baby spinach in a mustard vinaigrette, and a glass of cold white wine.

MAKE AHEAD
This dish can be partially prepared the night before it is cooked. Complete Steps 2 and 3, returning mushrooms to sauce after it is thickened. Cover and refrigerate overnight. The next morning, brown turkey (Step 1), or if you're pressed for time, omit this step and place turkey directly in slow cooker stoneware. Continue cooking as directed in Step 4.

1 tbsp	vegetable oil	15 mL
2 lbs	skinless boneless turkey, cut into ½-inch (1 cm) cubes	1 kg
2 tbsp	butter	25 mL
1 lb	cremini mushrooms, halved or quartered	500 g
2	onions, finely chopped	2
4	stalks celery, peeled and cut into ¼-inch (0.5 cm) dice	4
1 tbsp	dried tarragon leaves	15 mL
1 tsp	salt	5 mL
½ tsp	freshly ground black pepper	2 mL
¼ cup	all-purpose flour	50 mL
½ cup	condensed chicken broth, undiluted	125 mL
½ cup	dry white wine	125 mL
1	red bell pepper, diced	1
½ cup	whipping cream	125 mL
8	frozen puff pastry shells	8

1. In a nonstick skillet, heat oil over medium-high heat. Add turkey pieces, in batches, and brown. Using a slotted spoon, transfer to slow cooker stoneware.

2. Add butter to pan and heat until melted. Add mushrooms and sauté until they begin to lose their liquid. Using a slotted spoon, transfer to slow cooker stoneware.

3. Reduce heat to medium. Add onions and celery and cook, stirring, until vegetables are softened. Add tarragon, salt and black pepper and cook, stirring, for 1 minute. Sprinkle flour over mixture and cook, stirring, for 1 minute. Add chicken broth and wine and stir until thickened (mixture will be very thick).

4. Pour mixture over turkey and mushrooms. Cover and cook on **Low** for 6 to 7 hours or on **High** for 3 to 4 hours, until turkey is no longer pink inside. Add red pepper and cream. Cover and cook on **High** for 20 to 25 minutes, until heated through.

continued on page 158

5. Bake pastry shells according to package directions. Fill with turkey mixture and serve piping hot.

TIPS
• I prefer the stronger flavor of cremini mushrooms in this recipe, but white mushrooms work well, too.
• Make your own puff pastry if you are so inclined, but using frozen puff pastry shells, which are readily available at the supermarket, makes this an easy weeknight meal.

PANTRY NOTES

Fresh Mushrooms
The many varieties of cultivated mushrooms, now widely available in supermarkets in both dried and fresh versions, are a great boon to cooks looking to add flavor and variety to recipes. Mushrooms, such as shiitake, oyster and wood ear, traditionally used in Asian cooking, are now adding diversity to many dishes. Cremini mushrooms used in this recipe have long been associated with Italian cooking. A more flavorful relative of the common white mushroom, they develop into meaty portobello mushrooms if left to mature.

All mushrooms are inclined to be delicate and should be treated with care. Mushrooms will keep for about five days in the refrigerator. They should be stored, unwashed, in a brown paper bag rather than a plastic bag, which allows them to breathe. Before being used, they should be gently cleaned. Rinse under running water and immediately pat dry or simply wipe with a damp paper towel.

Best-Ever Turkey Breast

SERVES 4 TO 6

....

*If you want to celebrate
a holiday with turkey
but don't feel like cooking
an entire bird, try this
tasty alternative.
Accompany with roast or
mashed potatoes,
Brussels sprouts and
cranberry ketchup for a
great festive meal.*

2	slices bacon	2
1	turkey breast, skin on about 2 to 3 lbs (1 to 1.5 kg)	1
2 tbsp	brandy or cognac, optional	25 mL
2	onions, finely chopped	2
4	carrots, peeled and diced	4
4	stalks celery, peeled and diced	4
2	cloves garlic, minced	2
1 tsp	ground sage	5 mL
6	whole cloves or allspice	6
1 tsp	salt	5 mL
½ tsp	cracked black peppercorns	2 mL
¼ cup	all-purpose flour	50 mL
¾ cup	dry white wine or chicken broth	175 mL

MAKE AHEAD
This dish can be partially prepared the night before it is cooked. Complete Steps 1 and 3. Cover and refrigerate overnight. The next morning, brown turkey breast (Step 2), or if you're pressed for time, remove skin from turkey breast, omit browning and place directly in slow cooker stoneware. Omit the optional brandy flambé. Continue cooking as directed in Step 4.

1. In a skillet, cook bacon over medium-high heat until crisp. Remove from pan and drain on paper towel. Crumble and set aside. Drain all but 2 tbsp (25 mL) fat from pan.

2. Add turkey breast to pan and brown on all sides. Turn turkey skin side up and sprinkle with brandy, if using. Ignite, stand back and wait for flames to subside. Transfer to slow cooker stoneware.

3. Add onion, carrots and celery to pan and cook, stirring, until vegetables are softened. Add garlic, sage, cloves, salt and peppercorns and cook, stirring, for 1 minute. Sprinkle flour over mixture and cook, stirring, for 1 minute. Stir in reserved bacon and wine and cook until mixture thickens.

4. Spoon sauce over turkey breast. Cover and cook on **Low** for 6 to 8 hours or on **High** for 3 to 4 hours, until turkey is tender and no longer pink inside or an instant-read meat thermometer reads 170°F (80°C). Transfer turkey to a warm platter, spoon sauce over and serve piping hot.

Fish and Seafood

Mussels in Lemongrass Tomato Broth

Mussels in Lemongrass Tomato Broth

SERVES 4 AS A MAIN COURSE OR 6 AS A STARTER

....

This is a variation of a recipe that appeared in New World Noodles *by Bill Jones and Stephen Wong. I particularly enjoy the unusual and slightly Indonesian flavors of the delicious broth. This works equally well as the centerpiece of a light meal or as a dramatic first course.*

MAKE AHEAD
This dish can be partially prepared ahead of time. Complete Step 1. Cover and refrigerate broth until ready to use, then proceed with Step 2.

1 tbsp	vegetable oil	15 mL
1	onion, finely chopped	1
2	cloves garlic, minced	2
1 tsp	gingerroot, minced	5 mL
1 tsp	coriander seeds	5 mL
1	cinnamon stick piece, about 2 inches (5 cm)	1
1	stalk lemongrass, coarsely chopped	1
½ tsp	salt	2 mL
½ tsp	whole black peppercorns	2 mL
1	can (28 oz/796 mL) plum tomatoes, including juice, chopped	1
2 cups	vegetable stock, or 1 cup (250 mL) clam juice mixed with 1 cup (250 mL) water	500 mL
3 lbs	mussels, cleaned (see Tip, below)	1.5 kg
	Finely chopped cilantro	
	Hot pepper sauce, optional	

1. In a skillet, heat oil over medium heat. Add onion and cook, stirring, until softened. Add garlic, gingerroot, coriander seeds, cinnamon stick, lemongrass, salt and peppercorns and cook, stirring, for 1 minute. Add tomatoes and vegetable stock and bring to a boil. Cover and cook on **Low** for 8 to 10 hours or on **High** for 4 to 5 hours. Strain broth through a fine-mesh strainer, pressing out liquid with a wooden spoon.

2. Transfer strained broth to a large saucepan and bring to a boil. Add mussels, cover and cook until mussels open. Discard any that do not open. Ladle mussels and broth into bowls, garnish with cilantro and serve. Pass hot pepper sauce, if desired.

....

TIP
• Farmed mussels are very clean and only need to be thoroughly rinsed under water before use in this recipe. If the mussels are not farmed, they will need to be carefully scrubbed with a wire brush under cold running water. Any fibrous beard should be trimmed with a sharp knife. The mussels should be tightly closed, or they should close when you tap them. If not, discard before cooking. Discard any that do not open after they are cooked.

Savory Vegetable Stew with Chili-Crusted Halibut

SERVES 4 TO 6

This tasty stew is a meal in itself. All it needs is crusty bread to soak up the sauce.

MAKE AHEAD
This dish can be partially prepared the night before it is cooked. Complete Step 1. Cover and refrigerate overnight. The next day continue cooking as directed.

2	onions, finely chopped	2
2	carrots, peeled and finely chopped	2
2	potatoes, cut into ¼-inch (0.5 cm) dice	2
1 tsp	dried oregano leaves	5 mL
1 tsp	salt	5 mL
¼ tsp	freshly ground black pepper	1 mL
2 cups	bottled clam juice	500 mL
2 cups	dry white wine	500 mL
2 cups	water	500 mL
1 tbsp	lime juice	15 mL
1	green bell pepper, chopped	1
1 cup	buttermilk (see Tip, below)	250 mL
½ cup	cornmeal	125 mL
1 tsp	chili powder	5 mL
1½ lbs	halibut fillets, cut into ½-inch (1 cm) squares	750 g
2 tbsp	vegetable oil	25 mL

1. In slow cooker stoneware, combine onions, carrots, potatoes, oregano, salt, black pepper, clam juice, white wine, water and lime juice.

2. Cover and cook on **Low** for 8 to 10 hours or on **High** for 4 to 5 hours, until vegetables are tender. Stir in green pepper and buttermilk. Cover and cook on **High** for 20 minutes or until pepper is soft.

3. In a plastic bag, combine cornmeal and chili powder. Add halibut and toss until evenly coated. In a nonstick skillet, heat oil over medium-high heat. Add fish and sauté, turning once.

4. Place fish in bowl. Ladle stew over top.

TIP
• If you don't have buttermilk, mix ¾ cup (175 mL) milk with 3 tbsp (45 mL) sour cream.

Portuguese Sausage and Shellfish Stew

SERVES 6

This robust Portuguese-inspired dish is easy to make, yet produces impressive results. I like to serve this with a big green salad, hot Portuguese cornbread and a crisp white wine.

MAKE AHEAD
This dish can be partially prepared the night before it is cooked. Complete Step 1. Cover and refrigerate mixture overnight. The next morning, continue with Step 2.

1 lb	soft chorizo sausage, removed from casings	500 g
4	stalks celery, peeled and thinly sliced	4
4	cloves garlic, minced	4
1 tsp	paprika	5 mL
¼ tsp	salt	1 mL
¼ tsp	cracked black peppercorns	1 mL
Pinch	saffron threads, soaked in ¼ cup (50 mL) boiling water, optional	Pinch
2 cups	dry white wine	500 mL
2 cups	tomato sauce	500 mL
½ cup	bottled clam juice	125 mL
½ cup	water	125 mL
1	green bell pepper, finely chopped	1
1 lb	medium shrimp	500 g
12	mussels or small clams (see Tips, page 166)	12
	Finely chopped fresh parsley	

1. In a nonstick skillet, cook chorizo and celery over medium heat, until sausage is no longer pink. Add garlic, paprika, salt, peppercorns and saffron, if using, and cook, stirring, for 1 minute. Using a slotted spoon, transfer to slow cooker stoneware. Add wine, tomato sauce, clam juice and water and stir well.

2. Cover and cook on **Low** for 6 to 8 hours or on **High** for 3 to 4 hours, until hot and bubbling.

3. In a large pot of boiling salted water, immerse shrimp, in shells. Cook over **High** heat until the shells turn pink, about 2 to 3 minutes. Allow to cool, then peel and devein.

4. Add green pepper and shrimp to contents of slow cooker and stir to combine. Lay cleaned mussels on top of mixture and spoon hot liquid over them. (If using clams, see Tips, page 166.) Cover and cook on **High** for 20 minutes, until mussels have opened. Discard any mussels that do not open. Garnish liberally with parsley and serve in big bowls.

continued on page 166

TIPS

• Farmed mussels are preferred for this recipe as they are very clean and only need to be thoroughly rinsed under cold running water before being cooked. If using mussels that have not been farmed, see Tip, page 162.

• Fresh mussels should be tightly closed or they should close when you tap them. If not, discard before cooking. Discard any that do not open after cooking.

• If using fresh clams in this recipe, clean clams first by scrubbing thoroughly with a wire brush and soaking in several changes of cold salted water. Discard any clams that are open. In a large saucepan over medium-high heat, bring $\frac{1}{2}$ cup (125 mL) of cooking liquid from stew to a rapid boil. Add clams, cover and cook, shaking the pot until all the clams open. Discard any that do not open. Return clams, with liquid, to stew. Garnish and serve.

• If desired, substitute 2 cans (each 5 oz/142 g) baby clams, drained and rinsed, for the fresh clams.

Florida Fish Chowder

SERVES 6 TO 8

Served with salad and crusty bread, this simple fish chowder can be the basis of a delicious light meal. If you prefer a creamier or less peppery version, drizzle with cream.

MAKE AHEAD
This dish can be partially prepared the night before it is served. Complete Step 1. Cover and refrigerate overnight. The next morning, continue cooking as directed in Step 2.

2 tbsp	butter	25 mL
2	large leeks, white part only, cleaned and coarsely chopped (see Tip, page 203)	2
4	stalks celery, peeled and diced	4
2	carrots, peeled and diced	2
2	cloves garlic, minced	2
1	chili pepper, seeded and finely chopped	1
1/2 tsp	dried thyme leaves	2 mL
1 tsp	salt	5 mL
1/2 tsp	cracked black peppercorns	2 mL
2 tbsp	all-purpose flour	25 mL
1	can (28 oz/796 mL) tomatoes, including juice	1
1 tbsp	tomato paste	15 mL
4 cups	fish stock or 2 cups (500 mL) bottled clam juice plus 2 cups (500 mL) water	1 L
1 cup	dry white wine or water	250 mL
2	potatoes, peeled and diced	2
1 1/2 lbs	grouper fillets or other firm white fish (skinned), cut into 1-inch (2.5 cm) squares	750 g
1	green bell pepper, diced	1
	Finely chopped fresh parsley	

1. In a skillet, melt butter over medium heat. Add leeks, celery and carrots and cook, stirring, until softened. Add garlic, chili pepper, thyme, salt and peppercorns and cook, stirring, for 1 minute. Sprinkle flour over mixture and cook, stirring, for 1 minute. Add tomatoes and tomato paste, breaking up with a spoon, and bring to a boil.

2. Transfer mixture to slow cooker stoneware. Stir in fish stock, wine and potatoes. Cover and cook on **Low** for 8 to 10 hours or on **High** for 4 to 5 hours, until potatoes are tender. Add grouper and green pepper. Cover and cook on **High** for 20 to 30 minutes, until fish is cooked through. Garnish with parsley and serve hot.

VARIATION
Bermuda Fish Chowder: Add 2 tbsp to 1/4 cup (25 to 50 mL) peppered sherry along with the fish, depending on the amount of heat desired. To make peppered sherry, pour 1 cup (250 mL) sherry into a clean jar. Thoroughly wash 4 chili peppers, preferably Scotch bonnet, split in half and add with seeds to sherry. Cover and let steep for at least 24 hours. Strain the required amount into the chowder. Refrigerate the remainder and save for use in soups and stews, straining out the required amount as needed.

Manhattan Clam Chowder

SERVES 4 AS A
MAIN COURSE OR
6 AS A STARTER

....

Manhattan clam chowder is appealing because it is a lighter alternative to traditional New England-style chowder. However, I find that its tomato-based broth often seems harsh. The solution is to add a touch of cream. This creates a chowder with the zest of Manhattan and the creamy smoothness of New England — the best of both worlds.

MAKE AHEAD
This dish can be partially prepared the night before it is served. Complete Steps 1 and 2. Cover and refrigerate broth. When ready to serve, complete Step 3. In a saucepan over medium-low heat, bring broth to a simmer. Add clam cooking liquid and meat, cream and reserved bacon and heat through. Continue as directed.

1 tbsp	vegetable oil	15 mL
4	slices bacon	4
2	onions, finely chopped	2
2	stalks celery, peeled and thinly sliced	2
2	potatoes, diced	2
1	can (28 oz/796 mL) tomatoes, including juice, chopped	1
1 cup	bottled clam juice	250 mL
1 cup	water or dry white wine	250 mL
2½ lbs	clams, cleaned (see Tips, below)	1.25 kg
1 cup	whipping cream	250 mL
	Finely chopped fresh parsley	

1. In a skillet, heat oil over medium-high heat. Add bacon and cook until crisp. Drain well on paper towel, crumble, cover and refrigerate until ready to use. Drain all but 1 tbsp (15 mL) fat from pan. Reduce heat to medium.

2. Add onions and celery to pan and cook until softened. Add potatoes, tomatoes, clam juice and water and bring to boil. Cover and cook on **Low** for 8 hours or on **High** for 4 hours, until potatoes are tender.

3. Discard any clams that are open. In a large saucepan over medium-high heat, bring ½ cup (125 mL) water to a rapid boil. Add clams, cover and cook, shaking the pot until all the clams open. Discard any that do not open. Strain cooking liquid through a fine sieve. Using a fork, remove clam meat from shells.

4. Add clam cooking liquid and meat to slow cooker along with cream and reserved bacon. Cover and cook on **High** for 15 minutes, until heated through. Ladle soup into bowls and garnish liberally with parsley.

....

TIPS
• To clean clams, scrub thoroughly with a wire brush and soak in several changes of cold salted water.
• Substitute 2 cans (each 5 oz/142 g) baby clams, drained and rinsed, for the fresh clams, if desired.

Snapper and Okra Curry

SERVES 4

Here's a simple yet delicious fish curry. Although I have made it with snapper, this recipe will work well with any firm white fish.

MAKE AHEAD
This dish can be partially prepared the night before it is cooked. Complete Step 1. Cover and refrigerate overnight. The next morning, continue cooking as directed.

2 tbsp	vegetable oil, divided	25 mL
2	onions, finely chopped	2
2	cloves garlic, minced	2
1	long red chili pepper, seeded and finely chopped	1
2 tsp	turmeric	10 mL
1 tsp	ground cumin	5 mL
1/2 tsp	ground coriander seeds	2 mL
1/2 tsp	salt	2 mL
1/4 tsp	cracked black peppercorns	1 mL
1	bay leaf	1
1	can (28 oz/796 mL) tomatoes, including juice	1
8 oz	okra, trimmed and cut into 1-inch (2.5 cm) lengths	250 g
1/4 cup	cornmeal	50 mL
1/2 tsp	ground fennel seeds	2 mL
Pinch	salt	Pinch
Pinch	freshly ground black pepper	Pinch
1 lb	snapper fillets, cut into 1-inch (2.5 cm) squares	500 g
	Hot white rice	

1. In a skillet, heat 1 tbsp (15 mL) oil over medium heat. Add onions and cook, stirring, until softened. Add garlic, chili pepper, turmeric, cumin, coriander seeds, salt, peppercorns and bay leaf and cook, stirring, for 1 minute. Add tomatoes, breaking up with a spoon, and bring to a boil. Transfer to slow cooker stoneware.

2. Cover and cook on **Low** for 8 to 10 hours or on **High** for 4 to 5 hours. Add okra, cover and cook on **High** for 20 minutes, until tender.

3. On a plate or in a plastic bag, combine cornmeal, fennel seeds, salt and pepper. Add snapper and roll or toss until coated. Discard excess cornmeal. In a skillet, heat remaining oil over medium-high heat. Add dredged snapper and sauté, stirring, until fish is nicely browned on all sides and cooked to desired doneness. Ladle curry into a serving dish and layer snapper on top. Serve with hot white rice.

Halibut in Indian-Spiced Tomato Sauce

SERVES 4 TO 6

This robust fish recipe is almost a meal in itself. I like to serve it with fresh green beans and naan, an Indian bread, to soak up the sauce.

MAKE AHEAD
This dish can be partially prepared the night before it is cooked. Complete Step 1. Cover and refrigerate overnight. The next morning, continue cooking as directed.

2 tbsp	vegetable oil, divided	25 mL
2	onions, finely chopped	2
2	cloves garlic, minced	2
½ tsp	minced gingerroot	2 mL
1	long green chili pepper, seeded and finely chopped	1
2	whole cloves	2
2	pods white or green cardamom	2
1	cinnamon stick piece, about 2 inches (5 cm)	1
½ tsp	caraway seeds	2 mL
1 tsp	salt	5 mL
½ tsp	cracked black peppercorns	2 mL
1	can (28 oz/796 mL) tomatoes, including juice	1
2	potatoes, peeled and diced	2
¼ cup	all-purpose flour	50 mL
1 tsp	turmeric	5 mL
½ tsp	ground coriander seeds	2 mL
¼ tsp	cayenne pepper	1 mL
1½ lbs	halibut fillets, cut into 1-inch (2.5 cm) squares	750 g

1. In a skillet, heat 1 tbsp (15 mL) oil over medium heat. Add onions and cook, stirring, until softened. Add garlic, gingerroot, chili pepper, cloves, cardamom, cinnamon stick, caraway seeds, salt and peppercorns and cook, stirring, for 1 minute. Add tomatoes and bring to a boil. Transfer to slow cooker stoneware. Stir in potatoes.

2. Cover and cook on **Low** for 8 to 10 hours or on **High** for 4 to 5 hours, until potatoes are tender.

3. On a plate, mix together flour, turmeric, ground coriander and cayenne. Roll halibut in mixture until lightly coated. Discard excess flour. In a skillet, heat remaining oil over medium-high heat. Add dredged halibut and sauté, stirring, until fish is nicely browned and cooked to desired doneness. Spoon tomato mixture into a serving dish and layer halibut on top.

Poached Salmon

SERVES 6 TO 8 AS A MAIN COURSE OR 12 TO 15 AS A BUFFET DISH

....

Although I love salmon cooked almost any way, poaching produces the moistest result. The problem is, successfully poaching a large piece of salmon use to require a fish poacher, a piece of kitchen equipment that was rarely used yet relatively costly and cumbersome to store. A large oval slow cooker is the ideal solution. It produces great results, with little fuss. Serve poached salmon, warm or cold, as the focus of an elegant buffet or dinner, attractively garnished with sliced lemon and sprigs of parsley or dill and accompany with your favorite sauce. For a change that will challenge your palate, serve warm salmon with a tart sorrel sauce, one of my favorites.

MAKE AHEAD
Make the poaching liquid the day before you intend to cook. Cover and refrigerate until you are ready to use.

• *Large (minimum 5 quart) oval slow cooker*

Poaching Liquid

6 cups	water	1.5 L
1	onion, chopped	1
2	stalks celery, chopped or ½ tsp (2 mL) celery seed	2
4	sprigs parsley	4
½ cup	white wine or lemon juice	125 mL
8	peppercorns	8
1	bay leaf	1

Salmon

1	fillet of salmon (about 3 lbs/1.5 kg)	1
	Lemon slices	
	Sprigs fresh parsley or dill	

Sorrel Sauce, Optional

1 lb	sorrel leaves, washed thoroughly and stems removed (see Pantry Notes, page 174)	500 g
¼ cup	water	50 mL
½ tsp	dried tarragon leaves	2 mL
1 tsp	Dijon mustard	5 mL
¼ cup	whipping cream	50 mL
	Salt and freshly ground black pepper	

1. Poaching Liquid: In a saucepan, combine ingredients over medium heat. Bring to a boil and simmer for 30 minutes. Strain and discard solids.

2. Salmon: Preheat slow cooker on **High** for 15 minutes. Fold a 2-foot (60 cm) piece of foil in half lengthwise. Place on bottom and up sides of stoneware. Lay salmon over foil strip. Return poaching liquid to a boil and pour over salmon. Cover and cook on **High** for 1 hour. Remove stoneware from slow cooker. Allow salmon to cool in stoneware for 20 minutes. If serving cold, place stoneware in refrigerator and allow salmon to chill in liquid. When cold, lift out and transfer to a platter. If serving hot, lift out and transfer to a platter. Garnish and serve.

continued on page 174

3. Sorrel Sauce: In a heavy saucepan with a tight-fitting lid, combine sorrel, water and tarragon. Cover and cook over low heat until sorrel is wilted. Transfer sorrel and cooking liquid to a food processor. Add Dijon mustard and whipping cream and process until smooth. Season with salt and freshly ground black pepper to taste. Spoon over salmon, or pass separately in a sauceboat.

TIPS

• Make sure that the salmon is completely covered with the poaching liquid. If you do not have sufficient liquid, add water to cover.

• When the salmon is cooked, it should feel firm to the touch and the skin should peel off easily.

PANTRY NOTES

Sorrel

Although sorrel resembles spinach in appearance, it has a totally different taste, and the two cannot be used interchangeably. Sorrel is extremely bitter, but very flavorful. For a refreshing change, try adding a handful or two of sorrel to your favorite spinach soup. Although sorrel is increasingly available in supermarkets year-round, the best time to use sorrel is in the summer months when it is usually available at farmer's markets and is inexpensive. Sorrel is a hardy perennial, so if you have space, grow your own. When using sorrel, remove the stems and wash it carefully (see Tip for washing spinach on page 141).

Salt Cod Cassoulet

SERVES 6 TO 8

If your tastebuds have grown tired of the same old thing, try this tasty dish made with salt cod. Although this dried fish is not common in North America, it is a staple in Mediterranean diets and I love its flavor. On a recent holiday in Spain, I was fascinated to see food shop windows filled with big white slabs of this delicacy, obviously of various qualities, the subtleties of which were lost on me. In this recipe, the flavorful cod marries perfectly with the seasoned beans. Serve with a simple green salad, crusty bread and cold white wine for a delicious meal.

MAKE AHEAD
You can soak and cook the beans for this recipe while the cod is de-salting. Soak the beans for at least 8 hours, then cook overnight in the slow cooker. In the morning, continue with Step 2.

1 lb	salt cod fillets	500 g
2 cups	dried white navy beans, cooked and drained (see Make Ahead, left)	500 mL
6 cups	water	1.5 L
1 tbsp	vegetable oil	15 mL
2	onions, finely chopped	2
2	carrots, peeled and diced	2
2	stalks celery, peeled and diced	2
4	cloves garlic, minced	4
1	stalk fresh rosemary or 2 tsp (10 mL) dried rosemary leaves	1
1 tsp	salt	5 mL
½ tsp	cracked black peppercorns	2 mL
3 cups	vegetable or chicken stock	750 mL
½ cup	white wine	125 mL
	Juice of 1 lemon	
1	bay leaf	1
1 cup	whipping cream	250 mL

1. Rinse cod well under cold running water. Cut into five or six pieces and place in a large bowl. Cover with cold water and refrigerate for at least 24 hours, changing the water several times, until fish is softened and there is no trace of salt.

2. In a skillet, heat oil over medium heat. Add onions, carrots and celery and cook, stirring, until softened. Add garlic, rosemary, salt and peppercorns and cook, stirring, for 1 minute. Transfer mixture to slow cooker stoneware. Add beans, vegetable stock and white wine and stir well. Cover and cook on **Low** for 8 hours or on **High** for 4 hours, until vegetables are tender.

3. Drain cod. In a heavy pot with a lid, bring 4 cups (1 L) water to a boil. Add lemon juice and bay leaf. Add cod and cook until water almost reaches a simmer (it should not boil). Cover and remove from heat. Let fish stand for 15 minutes, until it flakes easily. Using a slotted spoon, lift out cod. Remove any skin, bones or dark pieces and flake cod into small pieces.

4. Add cod and cream to slow cooker. Cover and cook on **High** for 1 hour, until mixture is hot and bubbling. Serve piping hot.

TIP
• Salt cod is easy to cook, although it requires a long period of soaking with several changes of water. Planning ahead and cooking the dried beans in conjunction with soaking the fish can make this a relatively time-efficient recipe.

Meatless Mains

Cannelloni with Tomato Eggplant Sauce

Cannelloni with Tomato Eggplant Sauce

SERVES 8

Here's a great recipe for cannelloni that is remarkably easy to make. Oven-ready pasta is filled with ricotta and baby spinach and bathed in a tomato eggplant sauce. Add some crusty bread and a salad of roasted peppers or crisp greens for a terrific meal.

MAKE AHEAD
This dish can be prepared the night before it is cooked. Let tomato sauce cool before pouring over cannelloni. Refrigerate overnight in slow cooker stoneware and cook as directed.

Sauce

2 tbsp	olive oil	25 mL
1	medium eggplant, peeled, cut into 2-inch (5 cm) cubes, and sweated and drained of excess moisture (see Tips, page 183)	1
2	cloves garlic, minced	2
¼ tsp	freshly ground black pepper	1 mL
3 cups	tomato sauce	750 mL

Filling

2 cups	ricotta cheese	500 mL
½ cup	freshly grated Parmesan cheese	125 mL
1½ cups	chopped baby spinach	375 mL
1 tsp	freshly grated nutmeg	5 mL
1	egg, beaten	1
¼ tsp	salt	1 mL
¼ tsp	freshly ground black pepper	1 mL
24	oven-ready cannelloni shells	24

1. Sauce: In a nonstick skillet, heat oil over medium heat. Add eggplant, in batches, and cook until it begins to brown. Add garlic and black pepper and cook, stirring, for 1 minute. Add tomato sauce, stir well and bring to a boil. Remove from heat and set aside.

2. Filling: In a bowl, combine ingredients for filling. Using your fingers, fill pasta shells with mixture and place filled shells side by side in slow cooker stoneware, then on top of each other when bottom layer is complete. Pour sauce over shells. Cover and cook on **Low** for 8 hours or on **High** for 4 hours, until hot and bubbling.

TIP
• Be sure to use oven-ready cannelloni or manicotti in this recipe. It is a great time saver and it cooks to perfection in the slow cooker.

Tomato Mushroom Lasagna

SERVES 6 TO 8

Lasagna is a family favorite — in our house at least. Serve this vegetarian version with a tossed salad for a delicious and nutritious meal.

MAKE AHEAD
This dish can be prepared the night before it is cooked. Refrigerate overnight in slow cooker stoneware and cook as directed.

• *Large (minimum 5 quart) oval slow cooker, greased*

1 tbsp	vegetable oil	15 mL
4	large portobello mushrooms, cut in half and thinly sliced	4
2	cloves garlic, minced	2
1 tsp	salt	5 mL
½ tsp	cracked black peppercorns	2 mL
1 tbsp	freshly squeezed lemon juice	15 mL
3 cups	tomato sauce	750 mL
12	oven-ready lasagna noodles	12
2 cups	ricotta cheese	500 mL
½ cup	freshly grated Parmesan cheese	250 mL
2 cups	shredded mozzarella cheese	500 mL

1. In a skillet, heat oil over medium heat. Add mushrooms and cook, stirring, until they begin to release their liquid. Add garlic and cook, stirring, for 1 minute. Remove from heat and stir in salt, peppercorns and lemon juice. Set aside.

2. Spread one-quarter of tomato sauce over bottom of prepared slow cooker. Cover with 4 noodles, breaking to fit where necessary. Spread with half of the ricotta, half of the mushroom mixture, one-third each of the Parmesan and mozzarella. Repeat. Arrange final layer of noodles over cheeses. Pour remaining sauce over top and sprinkle with remaining Parmesan and mozzarella. Cover and cook on **Low** for 8 hours or on **High** for 4 hours, until hot and bubbling.

TIP
• Oven-ready noodles are a great time saver when preparing lasagna. Happily, the moisture generated in the slow cooker is a benefit when using this product, which in my experience works better in the slow cooker than in the oven, where the noodles can become a bit chewy.

Mushroom and Artichoke Lasagna

SERVES 8

I love the unusual combination of flavors in this lasagna, which reminds me of a Provençal gratin. In addition to adding flavor and color, the baby spinach is a great time saver as it doesn't require pre-cooking.

MAKE AHEAD
This dish can be prepared the night before it is cooked. Refrigerate overnight in slow cooker stoneware and cook as directed.

• *Large (minimum 5 quart) oval slow cooker, greased*

2 tbsp	butter	25 mL
1	onion, finely chopped	1
1 lb	mushrooms, trimmed and sliced (see Pantry Notes, page 158)	500 g
4	cloves garlic, minced	4
3½ cups	quartered artichoke hearts, packed in water, drained, or thawed if frozen	875 mL
¾ cup	dry white wine or vegetable stock	175 mL
12	oven-ready lasagna noodles	12
2 cups	baby spinach	500 mL
2½ cups	ricotta cheese	625 mL
2½ cups	shredded mozzarella cheese	625 mL
½ cup	freshly grated Parmesan cheese	125 mL

1. In a skillet, melt butter over medium heat. Add onion and cook until softened. Add mushrooms and garlic and cook, stirring, until mushrooms begin to release their liquid. Stir in artichokes and wine and bring to a boil. Cook, stirring, for 1 or 2 minutes, until liquid reduces slightly. Set aside.

2. Cover bottom of slow cooker stoneware with 4 noodles, breaking to fit where necessary. Spread with half of the ricotta, half of the mushroom mixture, half of the spinach, one-third each of the mozzarella and Parmesan. Repeat. Arrange final layer of noodles over cheeses. Pour any liquid remaining from mushroom mixture over noodles (see Tip, below) and sprinkle with remaining Parmesan and mozzarella. Cover and cook on **Low** for 8 hours or on **High** for 4 hours, until hot and bubbling.

TIP

• Unlike many recipes for lasagna, this one is not terribly saucy. As a result, the noodles on the top layer tend to dry out. Leave a small amount of the cooking liquid from the mushroom mixture behind in the pan, after adding to the slow cooker. Pour that over the top layer of noodles, particularly around the edges, where they are most likely to dry out.

Mushrooms and Eggplant Florentine

SERVES 4 TO 6

The addition of spinach, and therefore the moniker "Florentine," gives this fundamentally French gratin an Italian air. Rich and satisfying, all this needs is a tossed salad and a good baguette to complete the meal.

MAKE AHEAD
This can be assembled the night before it is cooked, without adding the spinach and cheese. Complete Steps 1 through 3. Cover and refrigerate overnight. The next morning, continue with Step 4.

1	large eggplant, peeled, cut into 2-inch (5 cm) cubes, and sweated and drained of excess moisture (see Tips, page 183)	1
1 cup	boiling water	250 mL
1	package (1/2 oz/14 g) dried porcini mushrooms	1
2 tbsp	oil	25 mL
2 tbsp	butter	25 mL
8 oz	cremini or button mushrooms, sliced	250 g
1	onion, finely chopped	1
2	cloves garlic, minced	2
1/2 tsp	salt	2 mL
1/4 tsp	freshly ground black pepper	1 mL
1/4 tsp	freshly grated nutmeg	1 mL
1	can (10 oz/284 mL) condensed cream of mushroom soup	1
2 lbs	fresh spinach or 2 packages (10 oz/300 g) spinach, washed, stems removed and coarsely chopped	1 kg
2 cups	shredded Swiss cheese	500 mL

1. In a heatproof bowl, soak mushrooms in boiling water for 30 minutes. Strain through a fine-mesh sieve, reserving liquid. Pat mushrooms dry with paper towel and chop finely. Set aside.

2. In a nonstick skillet, heat oil over medium heat. Add sweated eggplant, in batches, and cook until browned. Transfer to slow cooker stoneware.

3. Add butter to pan and cook fresh mushrooms, stirring, until they lose their liquid. Transfer to slow cooker stoneware. Add onions to pan and cook, stirring, until softened. Add garlic, salt, black pepper, nutmeg and reserved mushrooms and cook, stirring, for 1 minute. Add soup and reserved soaking liquid from dried mushrooms and stir until mixture is smooth. Transfer mixture to stoneware and stir well.

4. Cover and cook on **Low** for 8 hours or on **High** for 4 hours, until hot and bubbling. Stir spinach into mixture and sprinkle cheese over top. Cover and cook on **High** for 20 minutes, until spinach is cooked and cheese is melted.

Eggplant and Potato Curry

SERVES 6

This delicious curry is a great centerpiece for a vegetarian meal. Make an effort to find tomato chutney, which can be difficult to locate, as it is the perfect finish to this ambrosial stew.

MAKE AHEAD
This dish can be assembled the night before it is cooked. Complete Steps 1 and 2. Cover and refrigerate overnight. The next morning, continue with Step 3.

2	medium eggplants, peeled, cut into 2-inch (5 cm) cubes, and sweated and drained of excess moisture (see Tips, below)	2
2 tbsp	vegetable oil (approx.)	25 mL
2	onions, finely chopped	2
2	cloves garlic, minced	2
1 tsp	minced gingerroot	5 mL
1	long red chili pepper, finely chopped, optional	1
2 tsp	curry powder	10 mL
½ tsp	salt	2 mL
½ tsp	cracked black peppercorns	2 mL
1 tbsp	tomato paste	15 mL
1 cup	water	250 mL
2	potatoes, peeled and diced	2
	Tomato chutney (see Tips, below)	

1. In a nonstick skillet, heat oil over medium heat. Add sweated eggplant, in batches, and cook until browned. Transfer to slow cooker stoneware.

2. Add onions to pan, adding 1 tbsp (15 mL) oil if necessary, and cook, stirring, until softened. Add garlic, gingerroot, chili, if using, curry powder, salt and peppercorns and cook, stirring, for 1 minute. Stir in tomato paste and water. Pour mixture over eggplant in slow cooker stoneware.

3. Add potatoes and stir to combine. Cover and cook on **Low** for 8 hours or on **High** for 4 hours, until hot and bubbling. Stir in tomato chutney to taste, or pass at the table.

TIPS
• If you can't find tomato chutney, use tomato-based chili sauce instead.
• Although eggplant is delicious when properly cooked, some varieties tend to be bitter. Since the bitterness is concentrated under the skin, I peel eggplant before using. Sprinkling the pieces with salt and leaving them to "sweat" for an hour or two also draws out the bitter juice. If time is short, blanch the pieces for a minute or two in heavily salted water. In either case, rinse thoroughly in fresh cold water and, using your hands, squeeze out the excess moisture. Pat dry with paper towels and it's ready for cooking.

Cheesy White Chili with Cauliflower

SERVES 6 TO 8

This pale vegetarian chili is both pretty to look at and delicious to eat. Add the cream cheese if you prefer a thicker, cheesier sauce, and the mild green chilies for a flavor boost. Serve with hot crusty bread and a salad of sliced tomatoes in vinaigrette for a great meal.

MAKE AHEAD
This chili can be partially prepared the night before it is cooked. Complete Step 1. Cover and refrigerate overnight. The next morning, continue cooking as directed.

1 tbsp	vegetable oil	15 mL
2	onions, finely chopped	2
4	cloves garlic, minced	4
1 to 2	jalapeño peppers, minced	1 to 2
1 tbsp	cumin seeds	15 mL
1 tbsp	dried oregano leaves	15 mL
1 tbsp	chili powder	15 mL
1 tsp	salt	5 mL
1/2 tsp	cracked black peppercorns	2 mL
1	can (19 oz/540 mL) white kidney beans, drained and rinsed, or 1 cup (250 mL) dried white kidney beans, cooked and drained (see Basic Beans, page 214)	1
3 cups	vegetable stock	750 mL
3 cups	cauliflower florets, cooked for 4 minutes in salted boiling water and drained	750 mL
1	green bell pepper, cut into thin strips	1
2 cups	shredded Monterey Jack cheese	500 mL
4 oz	cream cheese, cut into 1/2-inch (1 cm) cubes, optional	125 g
1	can (4.5 oz/127 mL) chopped mild green chilies, optional	1
	Finely chopped green onions, optional	
	Finely chopped cilantro, optional	

1. In a skillet, heat oil over medium heat. Add onions and cook until softened. Add garlic, jalapeño pepper, cumin seeds, oregano, chili powder, salt and peppercorns and cook, stirring, for 1 minute. Transfer mixture to slow cooker stoneware. Add beans and stock and stir to combine.

2. Cover and cook on **Low** for 8 to 10 hours or on **High** for 4 to 5 hours, until hot and bubbling.

3. Stir in cauliflower, green pepper, Monterey Jack cheese, and cream cheese and chilies, if using. Cover and cook on **High** for 25 to 30 minutes, until green peppers are softened and cauliflower is heated through. Ladle into bowls and garnish as desired.

TIP
• If you prefer a thicker chili, mash some or all of the beans or purée in a food processor before adding to the recipe.

Three-Bean Chili with Bulgur

SERVES 10 TO 12

Here is a big-batch vegetarian chili so rich and thick your guests won't know it doesn't contain meat unless you tell them. The secret is the portobello mushrooms, which add meaty flavor, and the bulgur, which thickens the sauce and adds texture to the chili. Garnish with chopped avocado, sliced red onion, shredded Monterey Jack cheese and finely chopped cilantro for a tasty and healthy meal.

MAKE AHEAD
This dish can be partially prepared the night before it is cooked. Complete Steps 1 and 2. Cover and refrigerate overnight. The next morning, continue with Step 3.

2 tbsp	vegetable oil	25 mL
3	large portobello mushrooms, stemmed and cut into ½-inch (1 cm) squares	3
2	onions, finely chopped	2
4	carrots, peeled and diced	4
4	stalks celery, peeled and diced	4
4	cloves garlic, minced	4
1 to 2	jalapeño peppers, seeded and finely chopped	1 to 2
2 tbsp	chili powder	25 mL
1 tbsp	dried oregano leaves	15 mL
1 tbsp	cumin seeds	15 mL
2 tsp	salt	10 mL
1 tsp	cracked black peppercorns	5 mL
1	can (28 oz/796 mL) tomatoes, including juice	1
3 cups	vegetable stock	750 mL
1 cup	dried white kidney beans, cooked and drained (see Basic Beans, page 214), or 1 can (19 oz/540 mL) white kidney beans, drained and rinsed	250 mL
1 cup	dried red kidney beans, cooked and drained, or 1 can (19 oz/540 mL) red kidney beans, drained and rinsed	250 mL
1 cup	dried chickpeas, cooked and drained, or 1 can (19 oz/540 mL) chickpeas, drained and rinsed	250 mL
1 cup	bulgur	250 mL

1. In a skillet, heat oil over medium-high heat. Add mushrooms and cook, stirring, until they begin to lose their juice. Using a slotted spoon, transfer to slow cooker stoneware.

2. Reduce heat to medium. Add onions, carrots and celery to pan and cook, stirring, until softened. Add garlic, jalapeño pepper, chili powder, oregano, cumin seeds, salt and peppercorns and cook, stirring, for 1 minute. Add tomatoes and bring to a boil, breaking up with a spoon. Pour mixture over mushrooms. Add vegetable stock, beans and chickpeas and stir to combine.

3. Cover and cook on **Low** for 8 to 10 hours or on **High** for 4 to 5 hours, until mixture is hot and bubbling. Stir in bulgur. Cover and cook until bulgur absorbs liquid and is tender, about 30 minutes. Serve hot.

TIP
• Like all chilies, this recipe reheats well. However, you can halve this recipe if the quantity is too large for you.

PANTRY NOTES

Dried Beans
This recipe showcases a variety of dried beans, which, in addition to being easily stored pantry ingredients, are one of our most healthful foods. Legumes, a category that includes lentils as well as dried beans, are a rich source of B vitamins, calcium, iron, phosphorous, potassium and zinc. They are also an excellent source of fiber and low-fat protein. Bulgur, a grain made from cracked wheat that has been roasted, completes the range of essential amino acids in the beans, making this a particularly nutritious dish for vegetarians as it is a complete protein.

Cider Baked Beans

SERVES 8

If, like me, you often have small quantities of several varieties of dried beans in your pantry, here is a great way to use them up. For a festive presentation, add the bread crumb topping. I like to serve this with a salad of shredded carrots and steamed brown bread.

MAKE AHEAD
To manage your time most effectively when making this dish, soak the dried beans overnight. Chop and peel the onions, celery, carrots, garlic and turnip the night before you plan to cook. Cover and refrigerate overnight. Measure the dried spices and cover. Combine apple cider, water and maple syrup in a 4-cup (1 L) measure. Cover and refrigerate overnight. The next morning, drain and rinse the beans and proceed with the recipe.

2 cups	assorted dried beans, soaked and drained (see Basic Beans, page 214)	500 mL
2	onions, finely chopped	2
3	stalks celery, peeled and thinly sliced	3
2	carrots, peeled and thinly sliced	2
2	cloves garlic, minced	2
2 cups	diced peeled turnip	500 mL
2 tsp	chili powder	10 mL
1 tsp	salt	5 mL
1 tsp	cracked black peppercorns	5 mL
4	whole cloves	4
1	cinnamon stick piece, about 2 inches (5 cm)	1
1 cup	apple cider or juice	250 mL
1 cup	water	250 mL
½ cup	maple syrup	125 mL
2 tbsp	cornstarch, dissolved in 2 tbsp (25 mL) cold water	25 mL

1. In slow cooker stoneware, combine ingredients, except cornstarch. Cover and cook on **Low** for 10 to 12 hours or on **High** for 5 to 6 hours, until beans are tender.

2. In a bowl, combine dissolved cornstarch with 2 tbsp (25 mL) hot cooking liquid from beans and stir until smooth. Gradually add up to ¼ cup (50 mL) hot bean liquid, stirring until mixture is smooth. Return mixture to stoneware and stir well until sauce thickens.

VARIATION
Baked Beans with Bread Crumb Topping: Preheat broiler. After beans are cooked, ladle them into individual heatproof tureens or a baking dish. In a bowl, combine 1 cup (250 mL) dry bread crumbs with ¼ cup (50 mL) each melted butter and finely chopped parsley. Sprinkle over beans and place under broiler until topping is lightly browned and beans are bubbly.

Two-Bean Chili with Zucchini

SERVES 6

Vegetarian chili, which is loaded with healthy vegetables and beans, is a great dish for those of us who are trying to eat less fat and increase dietary fiber. This delicious version combines fresh green beans with dried beans and adds corn kernels and sautéed zucchini for a tasty finish.

MAKE AHEAD
This chili can be partially prepared the night before it is cooked. Complete Steps 1 through 3. Cover and refrigerate overnight. The next morning, continue with Step 4.

2	small zucchini, cut into ½-inch (1 cm) lengths and sweated	2
2	dried ancho chili peppers	2
2 cups	boiling water	500 mL
1 tbsp	vegetable oil	15 mL
2	onions, finely chopped	2
2	cloves garlic, minced	2
1 tbsp	cumin seeds	15 mL
1 tbsp	dried oregano leaves	15 mL
1 tsp	salt	5 mL
½ tsp	cracked black peppercorns	2 mL
1	can (28 oz/796 mL) tomatoes, including juice, coarsely chopped	1
2 cups	green beans, cut into 2-inch (5 cm) lengths	500 mL
1	can (19 oz/540 mL) pinto or romano beans, drained and rinsed, or 1 cup (250 mL) dried pinto or romano beans, cooked and drained (see Basic Beans, page 214)	1
1½ cups	corn kernels	375 mL
1 cup	shredded Monterey Jack cheese, optional	250 mL
	Sour cream, optional	
	Finely chopped cilantro	

1. In a heatproof bowl, soak ancho chiles in boiling water for 30 minutes. Drain, discarding soaking liquid and stems. Pat dry, chop finely and set aside.

2. In a skillet, heat oil over medium heat. Add zucchini and cook, stirring, until it begins to brown. Transfer to a bowl with a slotted spoon, cover and refrigerate.

3. In same skillet, add onions and cook, stirring, until softened. Add garlic, cumin seeds, oregano, salt and peppercorns and cook, stirring, for 1 minute. Add tomatoes and green beans and bring to a boil. Transfer to slow cooker stoneware. Add beans and stir to combine.

4. Cover and cook on **Low** for 8 hours or on **High** for 4 hours, until mixture is bubbling and hot. Stir in corn and reserved zucchini. Cover and cook on **High** for 20 minutes, until zucchini is heated through. Ladle into bowls and top with cheese or sour cream, if using. Garnish with cilantro.

Rice and Bean Casserole with Cheese and Chilies

SERVES 6

....

Not only does this delicious casserole appeal to a wide variety of tastes, the combination of rice and beans creates a complete protein, making it particularly nutritious. Add a tossed salad and hot crusty rolls for a satisfying meal.

MAKE AHEAD
This dish can be assembled the night before it is cooked. Complete Steps 1 through 3. Cover and refrigerate overnight. The next morning, complete Step 4.

• *Greased 8-cup (2 L) baking or soufflé dish*
• *Large (minimum 5 quart) oval slow cooker*

2 cups	water	500 mL
¾ cup	long-grain brown rice	175 mL
1 tbsp	vegetable oil	15 mL
1	onion, finely chopped	1
2	stalks celery, peeled and diced	2
1	jalapeño pepper, finely chopped, optional	1
½ tsp	salt	2 mL
½ tsp	cracked black peppercorns	2 mL
1	can (10 oz/284 mL) condensed cream of celery soup	1
1	can (4.5 oz/127 mL) mild green chilies, chopped	1
2½ cups	shredded Cheddar cheese	625 mL
1	can (19 oz/540 mL) red kidney beans, drained and rinsed, or 1 cup (250 mL) dried kidney beans, cooked and drained (see Basic Beans, page 214)	1

1. In a saucepan, bring water and rice to a boil. Cover tightly, reduce heat to low and cook for 40 minutes, until rice is tender and water has been absorbed.

2. In a skillet, heat oil over medium heat. Add onion and celery and cook, stirring, until softened. Add jalapeño pepper, if using, salt and peppercorns and cook, stirring, for 1 minute. Add soup and stir until smooth. Stir in green chilies and Cheddar cheese and stir until cheese is melted and sauce is smooth.

3. In baking dish, combine cooked rice and beans. Add sauce and stir to combine. Cover tightly with foil, securing with a string.

4. Place dish in slow cooker stoneware and pour in enough boiling water to come 1 inch (2.5 cm) up the sides. Cover and cook on **Low** for 8 hours or on **High** for 4 hours, until hot and bubbly.

Rigatoni and Cheese

SERVES 6

Here's a comfort food favorite that works well in the slow cooker when made with rigatoni rather than the traditional macaroni. Serve with a tossed salad and crusty bread for a tasty family meal.

MAKE AHEAD
This dish can be partially assembled the night before it is cooked. Complete Steps 1 and 2. Cover and refrigerate overnight. The next morning, continue with Step 3.

• *Lightly greased slow cooker stoneware*

1	can (28 oz/796 mL) tomatoes, drained, reserving 1 cup (250 mL) liquid	1
1	can (10 oz/284 mL) condensed cream of mushroom soup	1
1 tsp	dried oregano leaves	5 mL
1 tsp	salt	5 mL
½ tsp	cracked black peppercorns	2 mL
3 cups	rigatoni, cooked until barely tender (7 minutes after water returns to a boil) and drained	750 mL
2½ cups	shredded Cheddar cheese	625 mL
½ cup	freshly grated Parmesan cheese	125 mL
½ cup	fine fresh bread crumbs	125 mL
2 tbsp	melted butter	25 mL

1. In a food processor, combine tomatoes plus reserved liquid, soup, oregano, salt and peppercorns. Pulse three or four times, until tomatoes are coarsely chopped and mixture is combined.

2. In slow cooker stoneware, combine rigatoni, Cheddar cheese and tomato mixture.

3. In a bowl, mix together Parmesan cheese and bread crumbs. Sprinkle evenly over rigatoni. Drizzle with butter. Cover and cook on **Low** for 8 hours or on **High** for 4 hours, until hot and bubbling.

Meatless Moussaka

SERVES 6

This delicious vegetarian version of the classic Greek dish, with an unusual tofu topping, is every bit as good as the original.

MAKE AHEAD
This dish can be partially assembled the night before it is cooked. Complete Steps 1 through 3. Cover and refrigerate overnight. The next morning, continue with Step 4.

¼ cup	vegetable oil	50 mL
2	eggplants, peeled, cut into 2-inch (5 cm) cubes, and sweated and drained of excess moisture (see Tips, page 183)	2
2	onions, finely chopped	2
4	cloves garlic, minced	4
1 tsp	dried oregano leaves	5 mL
1 tsp	cumin seeds	5 mL
½ tsp	salt	2 mL
½ tsp	cracked black peppercorns	2 mL
1	can (19 oz/540 mL) chickpeas, drained and rinsed, or 1 cup (250 mL) dried chickpeas, cooked and drained (see Basic Beans, page 214)	1
3 cups	tomato sauce	750 mL

Topping

1 lb	medium tofu	500 g
2	eggs	2
½ cup	freshly grated Parmesan cheese	125 mL
Pinch	each ground nutmeg and cinnamon	Pinch

1. In a skillet, heat oil over medium heat. Add eggplant, in batches, and cook until browned. Set aside.

2. Add onions to pan and cook, stirring, until softened. Add garlic, oregano, cumin seeds, salt and peppercorns and cook, stirring, for 1 minute. Add chickpeas and stir well.

3. Spread 1 cup (250 mL) tomato sauce evenly over bottom of slow cooker stoneware. Spread one-third of the eggplant over sauce and half of the chickpea mixture over eggplant. Repeat. Finish with remaining eggplant and pour remaining tomato sauce over top.

4. In a food processor or blender, purée ingredients for topping. Spread over eggplant. To prevent moisture from dripping on the topping, place tea towels over top of slow cooker stoneware (see Tip, page 236). Cover and cook on **Low** for 6 to 8 hours or on **High** for 3 to 4 hours.

TIPS
• If you are using a canned or bottled tomato sauce that is a little more or less than the quantity suggested, don't worry. Excellent results have been produced using as little as 2¾ cups (675 mL) to as much as 3¼ cups (800 mL) tomato sauce.
• Tofu comes in various textures. Soft or silken tofu works best in sauces, spreads and shakes. Firmer tofus will hold their texture in dishes such as stir-fries. Tofu in the mid-range of firmness works best in this topping.

Louisiana Ratatouille

SERVES 6

Eggplant, tomato and okra stew is a classic Southern dish, which probably owes its origins to the famous Mediterranean mélange ratatouille, a mouth-watering combination of eggplant, tomatoes, onions, peppers and often mushrooms and zucchini. Hence the name of this tasty variation. The secret to a successful result, even on top of the stove, is not overcooking the okra, which should be added after the other ingredients have melded.

MAKE AHEAD
This dish can be partially prepared the night before it is cooked. Complete Steps 1 and 2. Cover and refrigerate overnight. The next morning, continue with Step 3.

2 tbsp	vegetable oil	25 mL
2	medium eggplants, peeled, cut into 2-inch (5 cm) cubes, and sweated and drained of excess moisture (see Tips, page 183)	2
2	onions, finely chopped	2
4	cloves garlic, minced	4
1 tsp	dried oregano leaves	5 mL
1 tsp	salt	5 mL
½ tsp	cracked black peppercorns	2 mL
1	can (28 oz/796 mL) tomatoes, including juice, coarsely chopped	1
2 tbsp	red wine vinegar	25 mL
1 lb	okra, trimmed and cut into 1-inch (2 cm) lengths, about 2 cups (500 mL) (see Tips, below)	500 g
1	green bell pepper, cut into ¼-inch (0.5 cm) dice	1

1. In a nonstick skillet, heat oil over medium heat. Add eggplant, in batches, and cook, stirring, until lightly browned. Transfer to slow cooker stoneware.

2. Add onions to pan and cook, stirring, until softened. Add garlic, oregano, salt and peppercorns and cook, stirring, for 1 minute. Stir in tomatoes and red wine vinegar and bring to a boil. Transfer to slow cooker stoneware.

3. Cover and cook on **Low** for 8 hours or on **High** for 4 hours, until hot and bubbling. Add okra and green pepper. Cover and cook on **High** for 30 minutes, until okra is tender.

TIPS
• Okra, a tropical vegetable, has a great flavor but it becomes unpleasantly sticky when overcooked. Choose young okra pods, 2 to 4 inches (5 to 10 cm) long, that don't feel sticky to the touch (if sticky, they are too ripe). Gently scrub the pods and cut off the top and tail. Okra can also be found in the freezer section of the grocery store. Thaw before adding to slow cooker.
• An easy way to coarsely chop tomatoes while in the can is to use a table knife. Hold the knife vertically in the can and move from side to side, breaking up the tomatoes.

Vegetables and Grains

Collard Greens in Tomato Sauce

Collard Greens in Tomato Sauce

SERVES 6 TO 8

....

Collard greens, which are popular in the South, are a particularly tasty member of the kale family. Unlike most vegetables, they are very tolerant of long, slow cooking. Serve with hot cornbread to soak up the tasty sauce.

2	slices bacon	2
2	onions, finely chopped	2
2	cloves garlic, minced	2
1 tsp	salt	5 mL
½ tsp	cracked black peppercorns	2 mL
2 cups	tomatoes, coarsely chopped, including juice	500 mL
2 lbs	fresh collard greens, tough stems removed and chopped into 2-inch (5 cm) lengths (see Tips, below)	1 kg
	Hot pepper sauce, optional	
	Red wine vinegar, optional	

1. In a skillet, cook bacon over medium heat, until crisp. Drain on paper towel and crumble. Set aside. Drain all but 1 tbsp (15 mL) fat from pan and reduce heat to medium.

2. Add onions to pan and cook, stirring, until softened. Add garlic, salt and peppercorns and cook, stirring, for 1 minute. Add tomatoes and bring to a boil.

3. Place greens in slow cooker stoneware. Add tomato mixture and stir to combine. Cover and cook on **Low** for 6 hours or on **High** for 3 hours, until greens are tender. Serve with hot pepper sauce or a splash of vinegar, if desired.

....

TIPS
• You'll need 2 bunches of greens for this recipe.
• Collards require a thorough washing before being cooked. Soak the trimmed greens in several changes of tepid water, agitating to remove grit. Then rinse thoroughly, in a colander, under cold running water.

Leek Loaf

SERVES 4 TO 6

This creamy and delicately flavored loaf is particularly delicious served with grilled meats, poultry or fish. Accompanied by a tossed salad or a platter of sliced tomatoes in vinaigrette, it can also be the centerpiece of a light meal.

MAKE AHEAD
This loaf can be made ahead and refrigerated for up to 2 to 3 days until you're ready to serve. It reheats well in the microwave.

• *Lightly greased 4-cup (1 L) baking dish*

2 tbsp	butter	25 mL
4	large leeks, white part only, cleaned and thinly sliced (see Tip, page 203)	4
4	green onions, white part only, thinly sliced	4
2 oz	pancetta, coarsely chopped	60 g
¾ cup	table (18%) cream	175 mL
3	eggs	3
½ tsp	salt	2 mL
¼ tsp	freshly ground black pepper	1 mL
Pinch	freshly grated nutmeg	Pinch
¼ cup	shredded Swiss cheese	50 mL
2 tbsp	freshly grated Parmesan cheese	25 mL

1. In a skillet, melt butter over medium heat. Add leeks and cook, stirring, until softened. Transfer to food processor.

2. Add onions and pancetta to pan and cook, stirring, until onions are softened and pancetta just begins to brown around the edges. Transfer contents of pan to food processor and pulse several times, until mixture is well combined with leeks. Add remaining ingredients and pulse to combine. Spoon into prepared dish.

3. Cover dish with foil and tie with a string. Place in slow cooker stoneware and pour in enough boiling water to come 1 inch (2.5 cm) up the sides of the dish. Cover and cook on **High** for 3 hours or until a knife inserted in the center comes out clean.

4. When ready to serve, remove foil from baking dish. Run a sharp knife around the outside of the dish and invert onto a serving plate. Serve immediately.

TIP
• Bake this in a 7-inch (17.5 cm) square ovenproof dish, which fits very nicely into a large oval slow cooker. You can also use a round bowl or soufflé dish, but the cooking times will vary depending upon how the mixture is distributed in the dish.

New Orleans Braised Onions

SERVES 8 TO 10

....

I call these New Orleans onions because I was inspired by an old Creole recipe for Spanish onions. In that version, the onions are braised in beef broth enhanced by the addition of liquor such as bourbon or port. After the onions are cooked, the cooking juices are reduced and herbs, such as capers or fresh thyme leaves, may be added to the concentrated sauce. In my opinion, this simplified version is every bit as tasty. This is a great dish to serve with roasted poultry or meat. If your guests like spice, pass hot pepper sauce at the table.

2 to 3	large Spanish onions	2 to 3
6 to 9	whole cloves	6 to 9
1/2 tsp	salt	2 mL
1/2 tsp	cracked black peppercorns	2 mL
Pinch	ground thyme	Pinch
	Grated zest and juice of 1 orange	
1/2 cup	condensed beef broth, undiluted	125 mL
	Finely chopped fresh parsley, optional	
	Hot pepper sauce, optional	

1. Stud onions with cloves. Place in slow cooker stoneware and sprinkle with salt, peppercorns, thyme and orange zest. Pour orange juice and beef broth over onions, cover and cook on **Low** for 8 hours or on **High** for 4 hours, until onions are tender.

2. Keep onions warm. In a saucepan over medium heat, reduce cooking liquid by half.

3. When ready to serve, cut onions into quarters. Place on a deep platter and cover with sauce. Sprinkle with parsley, if desired, and pass the hot pepper sauce, if desired.

Sweet Potato Barley Risotto

SERVES 6

This delicious and unusual "risotto" is a tasty addition to almost any meal.

MAKE AHEAD
This dish can be partially prepared the night before it is cooked. Complete Steps 1 and 2. Cover and refrigerate overnight. The next morning, continue with Step 3.

1 tbsp	vegetable oil	15 mL
1	onion, finely chopped	1
2	cloves garlic, minced	2
½ tsp	dried rosemary leaves	2 mL
1	sweet potato, peeled and cut into ¼-inch (0.5 cm) cubes	1
1 cup	pearl barley, rinsed	250 mL
3 cups	vegetable or beef stock	750 mL
	Freshly grated Parmesan cheese, optional	

1. In a skillet, heat oil over medium heat. Add onion and cook, stirring, until softened. Add garlic and rosemary and cook, stirring, for 1 minute. Stir in barley until well coated with mixture. Add stock and bring to a boil.

2. Place sweet potato in slow cooker stoneware. Cover with barley mixture and stir to combine.

3. Cover and cook on **Low** for 8 hours or on **High** for 4 hours, until barley and sweet potato are tender. Stir in Parmesan, if using, and serve immediately.

Leek and Barley Risotto

SERVES 8

Here's another interesting barley "risotto," which makes a good accompaniment to many dishes. It can also be the centerpiece of a vegetarian meal, served with a salad and hot, crusty bread.

MAKE AHEAD
This dish can be partially prepared the night before it is cooked. Complete Step 1. Cover and refrigerate overnight. The next morning, continue with Step 2.

1 tbsp	vegetable oil	15 mL
3	leeks, white part only, cleaned and thinly sliced (see Tip, below)	3
1 tsp	salt	5 mL
½ tsp	cracked black peppercorns	2 mL
2 cups	pearl barley, rinsed	500 mL
1	can (28 oz/796 mL) tomatoes, including juice, coarsely chopped	1
3 cups	vegetable or chicken stock or water	750 mL
	Freshly grated Parmesan cheese, optional	

1. In a skillet, heat oil over medium heat. Add leeks and cook, stirring, until softened. Add salt, peppercorns and barley and cook, stirring, for 1 minute. Add tomatoes and stock and bring to a boil. Transfer to slow cooker stoneware.

2. Cover and cook on **Low** for 8 hours or on **High** for 4 hours. Stir in Parmesan, if using, and serve piping hot.

TIP
• To clean leeks: Fill sink full of lukewarm water. Split leeks in half lengthwise and submerge in water, swishing them around to remove all traces of dirt. Transfer to a colander and rinse under cold water.

Hoppin' John

SERVES 8

This simple dish of beans and rice is traditionally served throughout the South on New Year's Day, often accompanied by greens with their flavorful cooking liquid, known as "pot likker." This slow cooker version keeps the tasty pot likker with the beans, eliminating the need for a second dish. I like to serve Hoppin' John as a light meal in bowls, like a vegetable stew, followed by a salad. If you prefer a drier version, which makes an excellent vegetable course or dish for a buffet, add another cup (250 mL) or two (500 mL) of cooked rice.

2 cups	dried black-eyed peas, soaked and drained (see Basic Beans, page 214)	500 mL
1	smoked ham hock	1
1 tbsp	vegetable oil	15 mL
1	onion, finely chopped	1
2	cloves garlic, minced	2
1 tsp	salt	5 mL
½ tsp	cracked black peppercorns	2 mL
1 tbsp	red wine vinegar	15 mL
1 cup	cooked white rice	250 mL
	Hot pepper sauce	

1. Place peas and ham hock in slow cooker stoneware.

2. In a skillet, heat oil over medium heat. Add onion and cook, stirring, until softened. Add garlic, salt and peppercorns and cook, stirring, for 1 minute. Pour mixture over peas. Add enough water to cover peas (about 4 cups/1 L). Cover and cook on **Low** for 8 to 10 hours or on **High** for 4 to 5 hours, until peas are tender.

3. Remove ham hock. Peel off skin and shred meat, if desired. Discard bone. (You can also discard the meat with the bone, depending upon your preference.) Taste cooking liquid and adjust seasoning, if necessary. Stir in vinegar and shredded meat, if using. Add rice and stir to combine. Serve with hot pepper sauce.

VARIATION

Hoppin' John with Sausage: This version makes a substantial main dish. After stirring in the vinegar and shredded meat, add 1 lb (500 g) thinly sliced smoked sausage such as kielbasa, andouille or hard chorizo and, if desired, a finely chopped green bell pepper. Cover and cook on **High** for 20 minutes, until sausage is heated through. Stir in rice (use more than 1 cup/250 mL, if desired) and serve with a tossed green salad.

Grits 'n' Cheddar Cheese

SERVES 6

I think I must have lived in the American South in a previous life because I'm absolutely crazy about grits. I could eat them for breakfast, lunch and dinner, which is unfortunate, because they can be difficult to find north of the Mason-Dixon Line. Serve this yummy pudding-like dish with grilled meat or shrimp and a tomato salad for a great meal.

• *Lightly greased slow cooker stoneware*

2 cups	water	500 mL
1 tsp	salt	5 mL
½ cup	grits (not instant)	125 mL
1 cup	milk	250 mL
½ tsp	freshly ground black pepper	2 mL
1 tbsp	butter	15 mL
2	eggs, beaten	2
1 cup	shredded Cheddar cheese	250 mL

1. In a saucepan, bring water and salt to a boil over medium heat. Gradually add grits, stirring until smooth. Remove from heat. Add remaining ingredients and stir to blend. Spread mixture evenly in slow cooker stoneware. Cover and cook on **High** for 4 hours, until set. Serve immediately.

VARIATION

Shrimp and Grits: Here's a quick and easy way to transform this recipe from a side dish into a delicious meal. To serve four people, peel and devein 1½ lbs (750 g) medium-size shrimp. In a nonstick skillet, heat 1 tbsp (15 mL) vegetable oil over medium-high heat. Add 2 cloves minced garlic along with the shrimp and cook until shrimp are just pink, about 3 minutes. Sprinkle with ¼ tsp (1 mL) cayenne pepper and 1 tbsp (15 mL) freshly squeezed lemon juice. Add 2 cups (500 mL) good-quality tomato sauce and cook, stirring, until bubbling. Spoon cooked grits (see above) onto a warm plate and top with shrimp. If you prefer, substitute ½ cup (125 mL) freshly grated Parmesan for the Cheddar cheese in Grits 'n' Cheddar Cheese.

Pot Likker Greens

SERVES 8

Here's another lip-smacking dish from the South. These soupy greens make a great one-dish meal. Be sure to serve lots of crusty bread to soak up the tasty liquid.

1	smoked ham hock	1
8 cups	kale or collard greens, tough ribs and stems removed and torn into 2-inch (5 cm) chunks (see Tip, below)	2 L
1 tsp	salt	5 mL
½ tsp	cracked black peppercorns	2 mL
4 cups	water	1 L
	Red wine vinegar, optional	
	Hot pepper sauce, optional	

1. In slow cooker stoneware, combine ingredients. Cover and cook on **Low** for 6 hours or on **High** for 3 hours. Remove ham hock. Peel off skin, shred meat and add to greens, if desired. Sprinkle with vinegar or hot pepper sauce, if using. Serve piping hot.

TIP

• Kale, a member of the cabbage family, is one of the prettiest vegetables. Dark green, with frilly leaves, it is a winter vegetable that supposedly benefits from an exposure to frost. It has a strong taste and reduces dramatically in volume when cooked. Like collard greens, it needs to be thoroughly washed as it is often quite gritty. Although it is fashionable to cook kale briefly, I find that it stands up well to a more traditional long, slow cooking.

Steamed Brown Bread

MAKES 1 LARGE LOAF OR 3 SMALL LOAVES, DEPENDING UPON THE CONTAINER USED

....

Served warm, this slightly sweet bread is a delicious accompaniment to baked beans. It also goes well with wedges of Cheddar cheese.

- *Three 19-oz (540 mL) vegetable tins, washed, dried and sprayed with vegetable oil spray, or one 8-cup (2 L) lightly greased soufflé or baking dish*
- *Large (minimum 5 quart) oval slow cooker*

1 cup	all-purpose flour	250 mL
1 cup	whole wheat flour	250 mL
½ cup	rye flour	125 mL
½ cup	cornmeal	125 mL
2 tbsp	granulated sugar	25 mL
1 tsp	salt	5 mL
1 tsp	baking soda	5 mL
1½ cups	buttermilk	375 mL
½ cup	molasses	125 mL
2 tbsp	olive oil	25 mL

1. In a bowl, mix together flours, cornmeal, sugar, salt and baking soda. Make a well in the center.

2. In a separate bowl, mix together remaining ingredients. Pour into well and mix until blended.

3. Spoon batter into prepared cans (in equal amounts) or baking dish. Cover top(s) with foil and secure with a string. Place in slow cooker stoneware and pour in enough boiling water to come 1 inch (2.5 cm) up the sides of the dish. Cover and cook on **High** for 2 hours, if using cans, or 3 hours if using a baking dish. Unmold and serve warm.

Carrots with Rice

SERVES 4 TO 6

Here's a tasty side dish that is easy to make. It's particularly useful as part of a festive meal as you can get it out of the way in the slow cooker, while you prepare the other dishes.

½ cup	water	125 mL
2 tbsp	long-grain converted rice	25 mL
1 lb	carrots, peeled and thinly sliced	500 g
2 tbsp	olive oil	25 mL
½ tsp	salt	2 mL
¼ tsp	freshly ground black pepper	1 mL
Pinch	granulated sugar	Pinch
	Lemon juice	
	Finely chopped fresh parsley	

1. In a saucepan, bring water to a boil. Add rice and return to boil. Cover, remove from heat and set aside while preparing the carrots.

2. In slow cooker stoneware, combine carrots, oil, salt, black pepper, sugar and rice mixture. Stir to combine. Cover and cook on **Low** for 6 to 8 hours or on **High** for 3 to 4 hours, until carrots and rice are tender. Add lemon juice to taste, and garnish liberally with parsley.

TIP
• For convenience, you can use peeled baby carrots in this recipe, if you prefer.

Slow-Cooked Polenta

SERVES 6

Polenta, an extremely versatile dish from northern Italy, is basically cornmeal cooked in seasoned liquid. It is one of my favorite grains. Depending upon the method used, making polenta can be a laborious process. This slow-cooked version produces excellent results with a minimum of effort.

- *6-cup (1.5 L) baking dish, lightly greased*
- *Large (minimum 5 quart) oval slow cooker*

3¾ cups	vegetable or chicken stock or water	925 mL
1 tsp	salt	5 mL
¼ tsp	freshly ground black pepper	1 mL
1¼ cups	cornmeal	300 mL

1. In a saucepan, bring stock, salt and black pepper to a boil over medium heat. Add cornmeal in a thin stream, stirring constantly. Transfer mixture to baking dish. Cover with foil and secure with a string. Place dish in slow cooker stoneware and pour in enough boiling water to come 1 inch (2.5 cm) up the sides of the bowl. Cover and cook on **Low** for 1½ hours.

VARIATION

Creamy Polenta: Substitute 2 cups (500 mL) milk or cream and 1¼ cups (300 mL) broth for the quantity of liquid above. If desired, stir in ¼ cup (50 mL) finely chopped fresh parsley and/or 2 tbsp (25 mL) freshly grated Parmesan cheese, after the cornmeal has been added.

Hot Breakfast Cereals

SERVES 4

Hot cereal is one of my favorite ways to begin the day, and happily you can use your slow cooker to ensure that all family members get off to a nutritious start. Cook the cereal overnight and turn the slow cooker to Warm in the morning. Everyone can help themselves according to their schedules. Thanks to my editor, Carol Sherman, who, inspired by the idea of waking up to ready-to-eat hot cereal, came up with the idea of adding rolled oats to multigrain cereal. For a crunchier version, use Irish oatmeal or steel-cut oats, instead of traditional rolled oats in either recipe.

- *These recipes work best in a small (maximum 3½ quart) slow cooker*
- *Well-greased slow cooker stoneware*

Hot Multigrain Cereal (pictured right)

1 cup	multigrain cereal, or ½ cup (125 mL) multigrain cereal and ½ cup (125 mL) rolled oats	250 mL
¼ tsp	salt	1 mL
4 cups	water	1 L
2	medium all-purpose apples, peeled and thickly sliced	2
¼ to ⅓ cup	raisins, optional	50 to 75 mL

1. In prepared slow cooker stoneware, combine all ingredients, except raisins. Cover and cook on **Low** for 8 hours or overnight. Just before serving, place raisins, if using, in a microwave-safe bowl and cover with water. Microwave for 20 seconds to soften. Add to hot cereal. Stir well and serve.

TIP

- Multigrain cereals are one way of ensuring that you maximize the nutritional benefits of cereal grains. You can buy them pre-packaged, usually in 3, 5 or 7-grain combinations or under a brand name, or you can make your own by combining your favorite grains. Store multigrain cereal in an airtight container in a cool, dry place.

Hot Oatmeal

1¼ cups	rolled oats	300 mL
½ tsp	salt	2 mL
4 cups	water	1 L

1. In prepared slow cooker stoneware, combine ingredients. Cover and cook on **Low** for 8 hours or overnight. Stir well and serve.

TIP

- Rolled oats, often called porridge when cooked, are probably the most popular breakfast cereal. For variety, try the variations called steel-cut oats, Irish oatmeal or Scotch oats, which have an appealing chewy texture.

Basic Beans

MAKES APPROXIMATELY 2 CUPS (500 ML) COOKED BEANS (SEE TIP, BELOW)

....

Loaded with nutrition and high in fiber, dried beans are one of our most healthful edibles. As a key ingredient in many of our best-loved dishes, they can also be absolutely delicious. The slow cooker excels at turning these unappetizing bullets into potentially sublime fare. It is also extraordinarily convenient — since discovering the slow cooker, I don't cook dried beans any other way. I put pre-soaked beans into the slow cooker before I go to bed and when I wake up, they are ready for whatever recipe I plan to make.

| 1 cup | dried beans or chickpeas | 250 mL |
| 3 cups | water | 750 mL |

1. Long soak: In a bowl, combine beans and water. Soak for at least 6 hours or overnight. Drain and rinse thoroughly with cold water. Beans are now ready for cooking.

2. Quick soak: In a pot, combine beans and water. Cover and bring to a boil. Boil for 3 minutes. Turn off heat and allow to soak for 1 hour. Drain and rinse thoroughly under cold water. Beans are now ready for cooking.

3. Cooking: In slow cooker, combine 1 cup (250 mL) presoaked beans and 3 cups (750 mL) fresh cold water. Season with garlic, bay leaves or a bouquet garni made from your favorite herbs tied together in a cheesecloth, if desired. Add salt to taste. Cover and cook on **Low** for 10 to 12 hours or overnight. The beans are now ready for use in your favorite recipe.

....

TIP
• This recipe may be doubled or tripled to suit the quantity of beans required for a recipe.

PANTRY NOTES
....

Legumes
Once cooked, legumes should be covered and stored in the refrigerator, where they will keep for four to five days. Cooked legumes can also be frozen. Packaged in an airtight freezer-friendly container, they will keep frozen for up to six months.

Storing Legumes
Dried beans and lentils should be stored in a dry, airtight container at room temperature. Since they lose their moisture over time, they are best used within a year.

Substitutions
Canned beans are a quick and easy substitute for cooked dried beans. For 2 cups (500 mL) cooked beans, use a standard 19-oz (540 mL) can. Rinse well under cold running water before adding to your recipe.

Red Beans and Rice

SERVES 6

This is a North American version of that classic combination of beans and rice, which turns up in many cuisines. Although it is a great side dish, it can do double duty as a main course, accompanied by a salad or green vegetable. If you prefer a more substantial dish and are not cooking for a vegetarian, add some shredded ham (see the variation, below).

MAKE AHEAD
This dish can be partially prepared the night before it is cooked. Complete Step 1. Cover and refrigerate overnight. The next morning, continue with Step 2.

1 cup	dry red beans, such as kidney, pinto, cranberry or romano, soaked, drained and rinsed (see Basic Beans, page 214)	250 mL
1 tbsp	vegetable oil	15 mL
2	onions, finely chopped	2
4	stalks celery, peeled and diced	4
6	cloves garlic, minced	6
1 to 2	jalapeño peppers, finely chopped	1 to 2
1 tsp	dried oregano leaves	5 mL
1 tsp	salt	5 mL
½ tsp	cracked black peppercorns	2 mL
3 cups	vegetable stock	750 mL
1	green bell pepper, chopped	1
1 tbsp	red wine vinegar, optional	15 mL
1 cup	long-grain white rice, cooked	250 mL
	Finely chopped green onion, parsley or cilantro	
	Hot pepper sauce, optional	

1. In a skillet, heat oil over medium heat. Add onions and celery and cook, stirring, until softened. Add garlic, jalapeño peppers, oregano, salt and peppercorns and cook, stirring, for 1 minute. Add beans and stir to coat. Transfer to slow cooker stoneware. Add vegetable stock and stir well.

2. Cover and cook on **Low** for 8 to 10 hours, until beans are tender. Add green pepper and vinegar, if using. Cover and cook on **High** for 20 minutes, until pepper is tender. Stir in rice, garnish with green onion and serve with hot pepper sauce, if desired.

VARIATION
Red Beans and Rice with Ham: Stir in 4 oz (125 g) shredded ham along with the rice.

Desserts

Rice Pudding with Cherries and Almonds

Rice Pudding with Cherries and Almonds

SERVES 6

This family favorite is delicious enough to serve at an elegant dinner party. Spoon into crystal goblets and serve warm or cold.

• *Lightly greased slow cooker stoneware*

¾ cup	granulated sugar	175 mL
½ cup	Arborio rice (see Tips, below)	125 mL
¼ cup	dried cherries (see Tips, below)	50 mL
2 tbsp	ground almonds	25 mL
1 tsp	grated lemon zest	5 mL
Pinch	salt	Pinch
4 cups	milk (see Tips, below)	1 L
2	eggs	2
1 tsp	almond extract	5 mL
	Toasted sliced almonds, optional	
	Whipped cream, optional	

1. In prepared slow cooker stoneware, mix together sugar, rice, cherries, almonds, lemon zest and salt. Whisk together milk, eggs and almond extract, and stir into rice mixture. Cover and cook on **High** for 4 hours, until rice is tender and pudding is set. Serve warm, garnished with toasted almonds and whipped cream, if desired.

   ....

   TIPS
   • Long-grain white rice can be successfully used in this recipe, but the pudding will not be as creamy as one made with Arborio rice.
   • Use 1 cup (250 mL) fresh pitted cherries in place of the dried cherries, if desired. Or substitute an equal quantity of dried cranberries, instead.
   • For a richer pudding, use half milk and half cream.

Maple Orange Pudding with Coconut

SERVES 4 TO 6

I love old-fashioned steamed puddings. For many years, these versatile treats fell into disfavor, likely due to their association with the ubiquitous suet puddings of Victorian times or the rich plum puddings, which many of us dutifully attack when stuffed to the gills with Christmas turkey. In fact, good steamed puddings, which most resemble a warm, dense cake, are delectable comfort foods. Serve this hot with vanilla custard or ice cream and expect requests for seconds.

- *6-cup (1.5 L) lightly greased pudding basin, mixing bowl or soufflé dish*
- *Large (minimum 5 quart) oval slow cooker*

1½ cups	all-purpose flour	375 mL
1½ tsp	baking powder	7 mL
½ tsp	salt	2 mL
½ cup	butter, softened	125 mL
¾ cup	granulated sugar	175 mL
2	eggs	2
½ tsp	vanilla	2 mL
2 tbsp	chopped candied orange peel	25 mL
2 tbsp	milk	25 mL
½ cup	flaked coconut	125 mL
2 tbsp	orange marmalade	25 mL
2 tbsp	maple syrup	25 mL

1. In a bowl, mix together flour, baking powder and salt.

2. In another bowl, beat butter and sugar until smooth and creamy. Add eggs and beat until incorporated. Stir in vanilla and orange peel. Add flour mixture and beat until just blended. Stir in milk. Blend in coconut.

3. In a small saucepan over low heat, stir marmalade and maple syrup until marmalade dissolves and mixture is smooth. Place in bottom of prepared dish. Pour batter over top. Cover basin tightly with foil and secure with a string. Place basin in slow cooker stoneware and pour in enough boiling water to come 1 inch (2.5 cm) up the sides. Cover and cook on **High** for 3 to 4 hours, until a toothpick inserted in center of pudding comes out clean. Unmold and serve warm.

TIPS

- Orange peel, which is used in fruitcakes, is available in the baking section of the supermarket.
- An English pudding basin is actually a simple rimmed bowl, most often white, that comes in various sizes. The rim is an asset as it enables you to make a seal with foil, which can be well secured with string or an elastic band.

Bread Pudding in Caramel Sauce

Nothing could be simpler than this delicious recipe for an old family favorite. Use leftover raisin bread for a more fulsome version. Serve hot or cold, depending on your preference.

• *Lightly greased slow cooker stoneware*

1½ cups	packed brown sugar	375 mL
¼ cup	butter, softened	50 mL
3	eggs	3
1 tsp	vanilla or 3 tbsp (45 mL) dark rum or whiskey	5 mL
1 tsp	ground cinnamon	5 mL
½ tsp	freshly grated nutmeg	2 mL
2½ cups	milk	625 mL
6	slices white bread, cut into 1-inch (2.5 cm) squares	6

1. In a bowl, beat sugar and butter until smooth and creamy. Add eggs, one at a time, and beat until incorporated. Add vanilla, cinnamon and nutmeg and beat until blended. Stir in milk.

2. In prepared slow cooker stoneware, place bread. Add milk mixture and stir to combine. Cover and cook on **High** for 4 hours.

PANTRY NOTES

Stale Bread
Throughout the ages, cooks have developed many different techniques for transforming stale bread into a delicious treat. Bread pudding, a common and much loved dessert, falls into this category. Often the bread is buttered and soaked in a flavored and sweetened milk before being baked. Frequently, fruits such as raisins or citrus peel are added to the mixture. In more elaborate versions, the bread is baked in an egg-thickened custard, often flavored with elaborate liqueurs. Properly made, all are delicious, and many people, including me, fondly remember bread pudding as a favorite childhood dessert.

Gingery Bread Pudding with Orange

SERVES 6

This easy-to-make yet delicious pudding is a great send-off for leftover bread. Try making it with whole wheat bread for a slightly crunchy and delightfully different result. Serve steaming hot with plenty of whipped cream flavored with vanilla.

• *Lightly greased slow cooker stoneware*

6	slices whole wheat or white bread	6
1/4 cup	butter, softened	50 mL
1/4 cup	orange marmalade	50 mL
1/4 cup	finely chopped candied ginger	50 mL
3	eggs	3
1/2 tsp	vanilla or 2 tbsp (25 mL) orange-flavored liqueur	2 mL
1/2 cup	packed brown sugar	125 mL
2 1/2 cups	milk	625 mL

1. Spread bread with butter and marmalade, then cut into 1-inch (2.5 cm) squares and place in slow cooker stoneware. Add candied ginger.

2. In a bowl, beat eggs with vanilla and brown sugar. Blend in milk. Pour mixture over bread and toss to combine.

3. Cover and cook on **High** for 4 hours, until pudding is set and edges are browning. Serve hot.

Cranberry Pear Compote

SERVES 4 TO 6

Oh so simple to make, this tasty and intriguingly seasoned compote is a refreshing finish to any meal.

1 cup	water	250 mL
½ cup	port wine, Madeira, or grated zest and juice of 1 orange	125 mL
½ cup	granulated sugar	125 mL
6	allspice berries	6
4	white cardamom pods, crushed	4
1 cup	cranberries, thawed if frozen	250 mL
4	large pears, peeled, cored and cut into quarters	4
	Fresh mint leaves, optional	

1. In a saucepan over medium heat, bring water, wine, sugar, allspice and cardamom to a boil. Add cranberries and simmer until they pop.

2. Transfer mixture to slow cooker stoneware and gently stir in pears. Cover and cook on **Low** for 6 hours or on **High** for 3 hours, until pears are tender. Chill well. Remove and discard allspice and cardamom pods and serve garnished with mint leaves, if desired.

Raspberry Custard Cake

SERVES 6

This is a delicious old-fashioned dessert. As it cooks, the batter separates into a light soufflé-like layer on top, with a rich, creamy custard on the bottom. Serve hot or warm, accompanied by a light cookie, with whipped cream on the side, if desired.

- *6-cup (1.5 L) lightly greased baking or soufflé dish*
- *Large (minimum 5 quart) oval slow cooker*

1 cup	granulated sugar, divided	250 mL
2 tbsp	butter, softened	25 mL
4	eggs, separated	4
	Grated zest and juice of 1 lemon	
Pinch	salt	Pinch
¼ cup	all-purpose flour	50 mL
1 cup	milk	250 mL
1½ cups	raspberries, thawed if frozen	375 mL
	Confectioner's (icing) sugar	

1. In a bowl, beat ¾ cup (175 mL) sugar with butter until light and fluffy. Beat in egg yolks until incorporated. Stir in lemon zest and juice. Add salt, then flour and mix until blended. Gradually add milk, beating to make a smooth batter.

2. In a separate bowl, with clean beaters, beat egg whites until soft peaks form. Add remaining ¼ cup (50 mL) sugar and beat until stiff peaks form. Fold into lemon mixture, then fold in raspberries.

3. Pour mixture into prepared dish. Cover with foil and tie tightly with a string. Place dish in slow cooker stoneware and add boiling water to come 1 inch (2.5 cm) up the sides. Cover and cook on **High** for 3 hours, until the cake springs back when touched lightly in the center. Dust lightly with confectioner's sugar and serve.

TIP
- I make this in a 7-inch (17.5 cm) square baking dish. The cooking times will vary in a differently proportioned dish.

VARIATION
Blueberry Custard Cake: Substitute blueberries for the raspberries.

Double Chocolate Raspberry Cheesecake

SERVES 8 TO 10

·······································

Here's a cheesecake to die for — a yummy white chocolate base, punctuated by luscious raspberries, resting on a rich chocolate crust. Even better, made in the slow cooker, it is virtually foolproof.

MAKE AHEAD
This cake should be made a day ahead and allowed to chill in the refrigerator overnight.

- *7-inch (17.5 cm) well-greased springform pan (see Tips, right) or 7-inch (17.5 cm) 6-cup (1.5 L) soufflé dish, lined with greased heavy-duty foil*
- *Heavy-duty foil, if using a springform pan*
- *Large (minimum 5 quart) oval slow cooker*

Crust

20	chocolate wafers	20
¼ cup	semi-sweet chocolate chips	50 mL
2 tbsp	granulated sugar	25 mL
2 tsp	melted butter	10 mL

Cheesecake

2	packages (each 8 oz/250 g) cream cheese, softened	2
½ cup	granulated sugar	125 mL
2	eggs	2
1 tsp	almond extract	5 mL
2 tbsp	amaretto liqueur or ¼ tsp (1 mL) almond extract, optional	25 mL
6 oz	white chocolate, chopped	175 g
¼ cup	whipping cream	50 mL
1 cup	raspberries, thawed if frozen	250 mL

1. **Crust:** In a food processor, combine chocolate wafers, chocolate chips and sugar. Process until fine. Transfer mixture to a bowl, add butter and mix well. Press mixture into the bottom of prepared pan. Place in freezer until ready for use.

2. **Cheesecake:** In a food processor (you can also do this in a bowl, using an electric mixer), combine cream cheese and sugar. Process until smooth. Add eggs, almond extract and amaretto, if using, and process until combined.

3. In a saucepan over low heat, combine white chocolate and whipping cream. Cook, stirring, until melted. Add to cheese mixture and process until smooth.

4. Arrange raspberries evenly over crust. Pour cheesecake mixture over top and cover tightly with foil (see Tips, right).

5. Place pan in slow cooker stoneware and pour in enough boiling water to come 1 inch (2.5 cm) up the sides. Cover and cook on **High** for 3 to 4 hours or until edges are set and center is slightly jiggly. Remove from slow cooker and chill thoroughly before serving.

TIPS

• To ensure that the cake lifts off the pan intact, spray pan with nonstick vegetable spray. For added insurance, cover the bottom of the pan with a parchment circle, cut to size.

• If using a springform pan, ensure that water doesn't seep into the cake by wrapping the bottom of the pan in one large seamless piece of foil that extends up the sides and over the top. Cover the top with a single piece of foil that extends down the sides and secure with a string.

Warm Orange Pudding Cake

SERVES 4

....

Here's a simple citrus-flavored pudding cake, with a soufflé-like top and creamy custard underneath. I like to serve this warm, abundantly garnished with whipped cream and fresh berries.

- *6-cup (1.5 L) lightly greased baking or soufflé dish*
- *Large (minimum 5 quart) oval slow cooker*

1 tbsp	butter, softened	15 mL
¾ cup	granulated sugar, divided	175 mL
2	eggs, separated	2
2 tsp	grated orange zest	10 mL
⅓ cup	orange juice	75 mL
2 tbsp	orange-flavored liqueur, optional	25 mL
3 tbsp	all-purpose flour	45 mL
¾ cup	milk	175 mL
¼ tsp	salt	1 mL
	Confectioner's (icing) sugar	
	Whipped cream	
	Fresh berries	

1. In a bowl, beat butter with ½ cup (125 mL) sugar until light and fluffy. Beat in egg yolks until incorporated. Stir in orange zest and juice and liqueur, if using. Add flour and mix until blended. Gradually add milk, beating to make a smooth batter.

2. In a separate bowl, with clean beaters, beat egg whites until soft peaks form. Add salt and beat until stiff peaks form.

3. Pour mixture into prepared dish. Cover with foil and tie tightly with a string. Place dish in slow cooker stoneware and add boiling water to come 1 inch (2.5 cm) up the sides. Cover and cook on **High** for 3 hours, until the cake springs back when touched lightly in the center. Dust lightly with confectioner's sugar and serve hot from the oven or just warm, with whipped cream and fresh berries.

Sweet Potato Pecan Pie

SERVES 8

....

I love everything about this mouth-watering dessert, which among its many charms, makes a great alternative to pumpkin pie. The gingersnap crust, the crunchy pecan topping and the creamy sweet potato filling are a delectable combination. Serve this hot or cold, with vanilla ice cream or whipped cream flavored with vanilla or brandy.

• *7-inch (17.5 cm) well-greased springform pan (see Tips, page 227) or 7-inch (17.5 cm) 6-cup (1.5 L) soufflé dish, lined with greased heavy-duty foil*
• *Heavy-duty foil, if using a springform pan*
• *Large (minimum 5 quart) oval slow cooker*

Crust

1 cup	gingersnap cookie crumbs	250 mL
3 tbsp	packed brown sugar	45 mL
½ tsp	ground ginger	2 mL
3 tbsp	melted butter	45 mL

Filling

2	medium sweet potatoes, cooked, peeled and puréed (about 2 cups/500 mL)	2
½ cup	packed brown sugar	125 mL
2	eggs, beaten	2
½ tsp	ground cinnamon	2 mL
¼ tsp	ground allspice	1 mL
Pinch	salt	Pinch

Topping

½ cup	chopped pecans	125 mL
¼ cup	packed brown sugar	50 mL
2 tbsp	melted butter	25 mL

1. Crust: In a bowl, combine gingersnap crumbs, brown sugar and ginger. Add butter and mix well. Press mixture into the bottom of prepared pan. Place in freezer until ready for use.

2. Filling: In a bowl, beat sweet potatoes, brown sugar, eggs, cinnamon, allspice and salt until smooth. Spread evenly over prepared crust.

3. Topping: In a bowl, combine pecans and brown sugar. Drizzle with butter and stir until combined. Sprinkle over top of pie. Place a layer of parchment or waxed paper over top of cake and cover tightly with a lid or foil.

4. Place pan in slow cooker stoneware and pour in enough boiling water to come 1 inch (2.5 cm) up the sides. Cover and cook on **High** for 4 hours, until filling is set. Serve warm or cold.

Pumpkin Chocolate Marble Cheesecake

SERVES 8 TO 10

This is a rich and delicious cheesecake that is easy to make in your slow cooker. The gingersnap crust and pumpkin-flavored cheesecake base accented with chocolate is an irresistible combination.

MAKE AHEAD
This cake is best made a day ahead and allowed to chill in the refrigerator overnight.

- *7-inch (17.5 cm) well-greased springform pan (see Tips, page 227) or 7-inch (17.5 cm) 6-cup (1.5 L) soufflé dish, lined with greased heavy-duty foil*
- *Heavy-duty foil, if using a springform pan*
- *Large (minimum 5 quart) oval slow cooker*

Crust

1 cup	gingersnap cookie crumbs	250 mL
3 tbsp	packed brown sugar	45 mL
½ tsp	ground ginger	2 mL
3 tbsp	melted butter	45 mL

Cheesecake

2	packages (each 8 oz/250 g) cream cheese, softened	2
¾ cup	granulated sugar	175 mL
3	eggs	3
1 tsp	vanilla	5 mL
¼ tsp	ground cinnamon	1 mL
¼ tsp	ground cloves	1 mL
¼ tsp	ground nutmeg	1 mL
½ cup	pumpkin purée (not pie filling)	125 mL
½ cup	whipping cream	125 mL
4 oz	semi-sweet or bittersweet chocolate, melted	125 g
	Chocolate curls	

1. Crust: In a bowl, mix together gingersnap crumbs, brown sugar and ginger. Add butter and mix to blend. Press mixture into the bottom of prepared pan. Place in freezer until ready for use.

2. Cheesecake: In a food processor (you can also do this in a bowl, using an electric mixer), combine cream cheese with sugar and process until smooth. Add eggs, vanilla and spices and process until incorporated. Add pumpkin and whipping cream and process until smooth.

continued on page 232

3. Pour mixture over crust. Pour chocolate over mixture, then using a knife, swirl to marbleize. Cover tightly with foil (see Tips, page 227). Place pan in slow cooker stoneware and pour in enough boiling water to come 1 inch (2.5 cm) up the sides.

4. Cover and cook on **High** for 3 to 4 hours or until edges are set and center is slightly jiggly. Remove from slow cooker and chill thoroughly, preferably overnight, before serving. Garnish with chocolate swirls.

TIPS
• To ensure that the cake lifts off the pan intact, spray pan with nonstick vegetable spray. For added insurance, cover the bottom of the pan with a parchment circle, cut to size.
• When melting chocolate for this or any recipe, take care to ensure that the chocolate doesn't "seize" and become grainy. To avoid this problem, grate the chocolate first by pulsing it in a food processor. Then melt in a double boiler over hot, not boiling, water, stirring constantly.

Cranberry Baked Apples

SERVES 6

Cranberries add a kick to this great old-fashioned dessert that never goes out of style.

½ cup	chopped pecans	125 mL
½ cup	dried cranberries	125 mL
⅓ cup	packed brown sugar	75 mL
¼ cup	melted butter	50 mL
1 tsp	grated orange zest, optional	2 mL
½ tsp	ground cinnamon	2 mL
6	apples, cored	6
½ cup	orange juice	125 mL
	Table or whipping cream	

1. In a bowl, combine pecans, cranberries, brown sugar, butter, orange zest, if using, and cinnamon. Using your fingers, pack filling into apples. Place in slow cooker stoneware. Pour in orange juice.

2. Cover and cook on **Low** for 6 hours or on **High** for 3 hours, until apples are tender. Transfer apples to serving dishes with a slotted spoon and spoon cooking juices over them. Pass the cream.

VARIATION

Granny's Baked Apples: For a simplified version of this recipe, eliminate the nuts and berries. Make a filling of ⅓ cup (175 mL) packed brown sugar, ¼ cup (50 mL) melted butter and ½ tsp (2 mL) ground cinnamon. Proceed as above.

Just Peachy Gingerbread Upside-Down Cake

SERVES 10 TO 12

The deliciously rich molasses-flavored gingerbread, topped with peaches in caramel, is an absolutely irresistible combination. Serve it with a big scoop of vanilla ice cream and savor every bite.

• *Lightly greased slow cooker stoneware*

¼ cup	melted butter	50 mL
½ cup	packed brown sugar	125 mL
2	cans (each 14 oz/398 mL) sliced peaches, drained, or 4 cups (1 L) sliced peeled peaches	2

Cake

2 cups	all-purpose flour	500 mL
2 tsp	baking soda	10 mL
½ tsp	salt	2 mL
1 tbsp	ground ginger	15 mL
1 tsp	ground cinnamon	5 mL
½ cup	molasses	125 mL
½ cup	boiling water	125 mL
½ cup	butter, softened	125 mL
1 cup	packed brown sugar	250 mL
1	egg	1

1. In a small bowl, combine butter and brown sugar. Spread over bottom of prepared slow cooker stoneware. Arrange peaches on top.

2. Cake: In a bowl, mix together flour, baking soda, salt, ginger and cinnamon. In a separate bowl, combine molasses and boiling water. In a mixing bowl, using an electric mixer if desired, beat butter and brown sugar until smooth and creamy. Beat in egg until incorporated. Add flour mixture alternately with molasses mixture, beating well after each addition. Pour batter over peaches.

3. Place tea towels over top of slow cooker stoneware (see Tip, page 236). Cover and cook on **High** for 3 hours or until a toothpick inserted in center of cake comes out clean. When ready to serve, slice and invert onto plate. Top with vanilla ice cream.

VARIATION
Apple Gingerbread Upside-Down Cake: Substitute 4 cups (1 L) chopped peeled apples for the peaches.

Cranberry Apricot Upside-Down Cake

SERVES 6

....

Keep cranberries in the freezer and dried apricots in the cupboard and here's a delicious cake you can make year-round from pantry ingredients. Serve with whipped cream or vanilla ice cream.

¼ cup	melted butter	50 mL
½ cup	packed brown sugar	125 mL
¼ cup	finely chopped walnuts or pecans	50 mL
1½ cups	cranberries, thawed if frozen	375 mL
¾ cup	chopped dried apricots	175 mL
Cake		
1¼ cups	all-purpose flour	300 mL
2 tsp	baking powder	10 mL
¼ tsp	salt	1 mL
¼ cup	butter, softened	50 mL
¾ cup	granulated sugar	175 mL
1	egg	1
1 tsp	vanilla	5 mL
½ cup	milk	125 mL

1. In a small bowl, combine butter, brown sugar and nuts. Spread over bottom of prepared slow cooker stoneware. Arrange fruit on top.

2. Cake: In a bowl, mix together flour, baking powder and salt. In a mixing bowl, using an electric mixer if desired, cream butter and sugar until light and fluffy. Beat in egg and vanilla until incorporated. Add flour mixture alternately with milk, beating well after each addition. Pour mixture over fruit.

3. Place tea towels over top of stoneware (see Tip, below). Cover and cook on **High** for 2½ hours or until a toothpick inserted in center of cake comes out clean.

4. When ready to serve, slice and invert on plate. Top with vanilla ice cream.

....

TIP

• To prevent accumulated moisture from dripping on the cake batter, place two clean tea towels, each folded in half (so you will have four layers), across the top of the slow cooker stoneware before covering. The towels will absorb the moisture generated during cooking.

Blueberry Semolina Cake with Maple Syrup

SERVES 6

This delicious cake, which is great for snacking as well as dessert, owes its origins to Greek cuisine. In Greece, cakes made from semolina, the durum wheat from which pasta is made, are traditionally soaked in flavored sugar syrup. This version simplifies the process by using maple syrup instead. Serve warm or at room temperature.

- *Greased baking dish or loaf pan (see Tips, below)*
- *Large (minimum 5 quart) oval slow cooker*

1 cup	durum semolina (see Tips, below)	250 mL
1 tsp	baking powder	5 mL
¾ cup	granulated sugar	175 mL
⅓ cup	butter, softened	75 mL
2	eggs, separated	2
1 tsp	vanilla	5 mL
¾ cup	plain yogurt	175 mL
1 cup	blueberries	250 mL
Pinch	salt	Pinch
½ cup	maple syrup	125 mL

1. In a bowl, mix together semolina and baking powder.

2. In a separate bowl, beat sugar and butter until smooth and creamy. Beat in egg yolks until incorporated. Stir in vanilla. Add semolina mixture alternately with yogurt, mixing well after each addition. Fold in blueberries. In another bowl, with clean beaters, beat egg whites with salt until stiff peaks form, then fold into batter. Spread mixture evenly in prepared dish and cover tightly with foil, securing with a string.

3. Place in slow cooker stoneware and pour in enough boiling water to come 1 inch (2.5 cm) up the sides. Cover and cook on **High** for 3 to 4 hours or until a toothpick inserted in center of cake comes out clean.

4. Turn out onto a serving plate and pour maple syrup evenly over top. Serve warm or allow to cool.

TIPS
- One challenge with making cakes in a slow cooker is finding a baking pan that will fit. I have made this recipe in both a 7-inch (17.5 cm) square baking dish and an 8½- by 4½-inch (21 by 11 cm) loaf pan with good results.
- For best results, put a layer of parchment paper in the bottom of the baking pan before adding the batter, to facilitate easy removal.
- Semolina is available at natural foods stores or supermarkets with a good selection of grains.

Meredith's Molten Blondies

SERVES 6 TO 8

....

A blondie is a brownie flavored with butterscotch instead of chocolate. This variation transforms that idea into a delectable dessert with cake on the top and sauce on the bottom. It is superb over vanilla ice cream. I have my daughter, Meredith, to thank for the idea of enhancing the recipe with chocolate chips, which are a great addition. Butterscotch chips or a combination of butterscotch and chocolate is equally delicious. This can also be served cold, with whipped cream.

1 cup	all-purpose flour	250 mL
1 tsp	baking powder	5 mL
½ tsp	salt	2 mL
2 cups	packed brown sugar, divided	500 mL
¼ cup	butter	50 mL
1 tsp	vanilla	5 mL
½ cup	milk	125 mL
½ cup	chocolate or butterscotch chips	125 mL
½ cup	chopped walnuts or pecans, optional	125 mL
1 cup	boiling water	250 mL

1. In a bowl, mix together flour, baking powder and salt.

2. In a separate bowl, beat 1 cup (250 mL) brown sugar with butter until creamy. Stir in vanilla. Add dry ingredients alternately with milk, beating well after each addition. Stir in chips and nuts, if using. Spread mixture evenly in prepared slow cooker stoneware.

3. In a heatproof measure, combine remaining brown sugar and boiling water. Pour over batter. Cover and cook on **High** for 2½ to 3 hours, until cake layer looks cooked. Serve warm with vanilla ice cream.

Italian-Style Cornmeal Cake with Orange

SERVES 6 TO 8

This is a delicious light cake. It makes a perfect finish to a great meal and is excellent to have on hand for snacking.

- *7-inch (17.5 cm) well-greased springform pan or 7-inch (17.5 cm) 6-cup (1.5 L) soufflé or baking dish, lined with greased heavy-duty foil*
- *Large (minimum 5 quart) oval slow cooker*

1 cup	fine cornmeal	250 mL
¼ cup	finely chopped walnuts or pecans	50 mL
2 tsp	baking powder	10 mL
½ tsp	salt	2 mL
¾ cup	granulated sugar	175 mL
½ cup	butter, softened	125 mL
2	eggs	2
1 tsp	vanilla	5 mL
1 tbsp	grated orange zest	15 mL
¼ cup	plain yogurt	50 mL

Orange Glaze, optional (see Tip, below)

½ cup	confectioner's (icing) sugar, sifted	125 mL
¼ cup	orange juice	50 mL
1 tbsp	orange-flavored liqueur, optional	15 mL

1. In a bowl, mix together cornmeal, walnuts, baking powder and salt.

2. In another bowl, beat sugar and butter until light and fluffy. Beat in eggs until incorporated. Stir in vanilla and orange zest. Add dry ingredients in two additions alternately with yogurt, mixing until blended. Spoon batter into prepared pan. Wrap securely in foil (see Tips, page 227) and cook on **High** for 4 hours, until cake is puffed and pulling away from side of pan. Glaze cake, if desired.

3. Orange Glaze: In a bowl, combine confectioner's sugar, orange juice and orange-flavored liqueur, if using. With a skewer, poke several holes in the cake. Spread glaze over hot cake.

4. Let cake cool in pan for 30 minutes, then unmold.

TIP
- Although the orange glaze is a nice finish to this cake, it is also very tasty without a glaze. Allow cake to cool, unmold and dust lightly with confectioner's sugar.

Chocolate Flan with Toasted Almonds

SERVES 6

....

Here's a deliciously decadent chocolate dessert. Save it for special occasions or treat yourself and enjoy.

- *6-cup (1.5 L) lightly greased mold or soufflé dish*
- *Large (minimum 5 quart) oval slow cooker*

Caramel

½ cup	granulated sugar	125 mL
2 tbsp	water	25 mL
1 tbsp	lemon juice	15 mL
¼ cup	toasted slivered almonds	50 mL

Flan

3½ oz	bittersweet chocolate, broken into chunks	105 g
1 cup	whipping cream	250 mL
1 cup	milk	250 mL
⅓ cup	granulated sugar	75 mL
2	eggs	2
2	egg yolks	2

1. Caramel: In a heavy-bottomed saucepan over medium heat, cook sugar and water until mixture becomes a deep shade of nutmeg. Standing well back from dish, add lemon juice and stir until bubbles subside. Pour into prepared dish and, working quickly, tip mixture around the dish until sides are well coated. Sprinkle almonds over bottom of dish and set aside.

2. Flan: In a heatproof bowl, place chocolate. In a clean saucepan, bring cream, milk and sugar to a boil. Pour over chocolate and stir until mixture is smooth and chocolate is melted.

3. In a bowl, beat eggs and egg yolks. Gradually add chocolate mixture, beating constantly until incorporated. Strain mixture into caramel-coated dish. Cover with foil and secure with string. Place dish in slow cooker stoneware and add enough boiling water to come 1 inch (2.5 cm) up the sides. Cover and cook on **High** for 2 to 2½ hours, or until a knife inserted in custard comes out clean. Remove and refrigerate for 4 hours or overnight.

4. When ready to serve, remove foil. Run a sharp knife around the edge of the flan and invert onto a serving plate. Serve with whipped cream, if desired.

Rich Chocolate Cake

SERVES 8 TO 10

I've been making versions of this cake for more than 20 years, and it is always a hit. It used to be a lot more work as it needed to be cooked twice — once in a water bath on top of the stove, then finished in the oven. Now, by using the slow cooker, it can be completed in one step. This is very rich, and all you need is a thin slice accompanied by vanilla-flavored whipped cream and perhaps seasonal fruit such as fresh raspberries or brandied cherries. Don't worry about leftovers as it keeps well in the refrigerator.

• *7-inch (17.5 cm) well-greased springform pan (see Tips, page 227) or 7-inch (17.5 cm) 6-cup (1.5 L) baking or soufflé dish, lined with greased heavy-duty foil (see Tips, below)*

8 oz	unsweetened chocolate (see Tips, below)	250 g
1 cup	granulated sugar	250 mL
½ cup	strong coffee	125 mL
1 cup	unsalted butter	250 mL
2 tbsp	brandy or coffee-flavored liqueur such as Kahlua, optional	25 mL
4	eggs	4

1. In a heatproof bowl, place chocolate. In a saucepan over medium heat, bring sugar, coffee and butter to a boil. Pour over chocolate, stirring until chocolate melts and mixture is smooth. Stir in brandy, if using.

2. In a separate bowl, beat eggs until they are lemon-colored. Gradually add chocolate mixture, stirring until blended. Pour into prepared pan. Cover and cook on **High** for 2 hours. Remove from slow cooker and chill overnight before serving.

TIPS
• If using a baking or soufflé dish, cover tightly with foil and secure with a string.
• For best results, make this with the best chocolate you can find.
• To ensure that the cake lifts off the springform pan intact, spray pan with nonstick vegetable spray. For added insurance, cover the bottom of the pan with a parchment circle, cut to size.

Apricot Almond Pudding

This variation on an old English pudding is rich and satisfying without being heavy. Serve with vanilla custard or ice cream for an unusual and delicious dessert.

- 6-cup (1.5 L) lightly greased pudding basin, mixing bowl or soufflé dish
- Large (minimum 5 quart) oval slow cooker

1½ cups	all-purpose flour	375 mL
¼ cup	ground almonds	50 mL
1½ tsp	baking powder	7 mL
½ tsp	salt	2 mL
1 tsp	ground ginger	5 mL
½ cup	butter, softened	125 mL
¾ cup	granulated sugar	175 mL
2	eggs	2
1 tsp	almond extract	5 mL
2 tbsp	milk	25 mL
¼ cup	dried cherries, cranberries or raisins	50 mL
2 tbsp	apricot jam	25 mL
1 tbsp	amaretto liqueur or liquid honey	15 mL
	Vanilla ice cream or custard	

1. In a bowl, mix together flour, almonds, baking powder, salt and ginger.

2. In another bowl, beat butter and sugar until smooth and creamy. Add eggs and beat until incorporated. Stir in almond extract. Add flour mixture in two additions alternately with milk, beating just until blended. Stir in cherries.

3. In a small saucepan over low heat, stir apricot jam and amaretto until jam is dissolved and mixture is smooth. Pour into the bottom of prepared dish. Spoon batter over top. Cover basin tightly with foil and secure with a string. Place dish in slow cooker stoneware and pour in enough boiling water to come 1 inch (2.5 cm) up the sides. Cover and cook on **High** for 3 to 4 hours, until a toothpick inserted in center of pudding comes out clean.

4. When ready to serve, run a knife around the edge of the pudding and unmold. Slice and serve with vanilla ice cream or custard.

Cranberry-Red Currant Crumb Pudding

SERVES 6

Don't discard that slightly stale bread. Here is another great recipe for transforming leftover bread into a delicious dessert.

- *6-cup (1.5 L) lightly greased pudding basin, baking or soufflé dish*
- *Large (minimum 5 quart) oval slow cooker*

2 cups	milk	500 mL
¾ cup	granulated sugar	175 mL
2 tbsp	butter	25 mL
2 cups	fresh bread crumbs	500 mL
3	eggs	3
1 tsp	vanilla	5 mL
¼ tsp	salt	1 mL
¼ cup	dried cranberries or raisins	50 mL
2 tbsp	red currant jelly, stirred until smooth	25 mL

1. In a saucepan over medium heat, bring milk, sugar and butter to a boil, stirring, until butter melts. Remove from heat. Stir in bread crumbs.

2. In a bowl, beat eggs, vanilla and salt. Stir in cranberries, then ¼ cup (50 mL) bread crumb mixture. Add remaining bread crumb mixture and stir to blend.

3. Place red currant jelly in bottom of prepared dish. Add bread crumb mixture. Cover with foil and tie tightly with string. Place dish in slow cooker stoneware and add boiling water to come 1 inch (2.5 cm) up the sides. Cover and cook on **High** for 2½ hours, until toothpick inserted in center of pudding comes out clean.

Apple Cranberry Upside-Down Cobbler

SERVES 6 TO 8

Impress your guests with this deliciously different cobbler, which unmolds beautifully on a platter. Serve with cinnamon or vanilla ice cream, or whipped cream.

• *6-cup (1.5 L) lightly greased, baking or soufflé dish*

4 cups	chopped apples	1 L
2 cups	cranberries, thawed if frozen	500 mL
¾ cup	granulated sugar	175 mL
1 tsp	ground cinnamon	5 mL
1 tsp	grated orange zest	5 mL
¼ cup	orange juice or port wine	50 mL
Crust		
1 cup	all-purpose flour	250 mL
2 tsp	baking powder	10 mL
½ tsp	salt	2 mL
1 tbsp	butter	15 mL
⅓ cup	milk	75 mL

1. In a bowl, mix together fruit, sugar, cinnamon, orange zest and juice. Pour into prepared baking dish.

2. Crust: In a bowl, mix together flour, baking powder and salt. Using your fingers, rub in butter until mixture is crumbly. Add milk, stirring, to make a soft dough. Roll out on a lightly floured board, or pat using your hands, to fit top of baking dish and place over fruit, pushing dough down the sides of dish to ensure that fruit mixture is completely covered. (You may need to discard a few spoonfuls of fruit so dough will fit flush with the top of the dish.)

3. Cover dish with foil and secure with a string. Place dish in slow cooker stoneware and add boiling water to come 1 inch (2.5 cm) up the sides. Cover and cook on **High** for 3 hours, until a toothpick inserted in center of topping comes out clean.

4. When ready to serve, run a knife around the edge of the cobbler. Place a serving dish or platter over the top of the dish, invert and unmold.

National Library of Canada Cataloguing in Publication

Finlayson, Judith
Delicious & dependable slow cooker recipes: created for Canada's kitchens / Judith Finlayson.

Includes index.
ISBN 0-7788-0052-0

1.Electric cookery, Slow.
I. Title.
II. Title: Delicious and dependable slow cooker recipes : created for Canada's kitchens.

TX827.F553 2002   641.5'884   C2002-901839-0

Finlayson, Judith
Delicious & dependable slow cooker recipes: created for America's kitchens / Judith Finlayson.
— US ed.

Includes index.
ISBN 0-7788-0060-1 (bound)
ISBN 0-7788-0053-9 (pbk.)

1. Electric cookery, Slow.
I. Title.
II. Title: Delicious and dependable slow cooker recipes : created for America's kitchens.

TX827.F553 2002a   641.5'884   C2002-902132-4

Index